I0538669

Maribel

Daughter of a King

A MEMOIR

Maribel: Daughter of a King

Copyright © 2025 by Maribel Cahill. All rights reserved.

All Rights Reserved. No part of this book may be used or reproduced in any manner whatsoever without the expressed written permission of the author.

The cover image, which also appears on the second-to-last page of this book, is titled *He Hath Made Every Thing Beautiful In His Time*. It is by Paige Payne and used with permission.

Paperback ISBN: 979-8-9927273-0-2
Hardcover ISBN: 979-8-9927273-1-9

Editor: Mary Beth Abel/Abel Editing
Cover Design and Interior Layout: Fusion Creative Works

Every attempt has been made to properly source all quotations.

Printed in the United States of America
First Edition

2 4 6 8 10 12

Table of Contents

Prologue

What is it that I most long to do?

I long to tell the story of my life—

Where I began, the path that was laid out before me,
the roads I took that brought me back

to where I am today.

The people I've met along the way—

those who stayed are the ones whose hearts and lives are
eternally linked with mine.

Those whose lives crossed my path for a season and left a mark
in mine, I'm grateful for

the lessons they've taught me.

I believe I am here still to teach lessons I have yet to impart and
to learn lessons

I have yet to learn.

It has been quite a journey, and I am grateful for whatever Time
I have left

to be the best I can be.

Here's my story . . .

When we've taught all we have to teach, when we've learned all we came to learn, given all we have to give and received all we have to receive, then it will be time for us to depart and return to the freedom of the spirit. But, for the present, we're here and we must embrace the physical if we're not only to survive but to become the best we can be.

Brenda Davies, MD
in *The 7 Healing Chakras: Unlocking Your Body's Energy Centers*

Introduction
The Dream

Everyone has a dream. Mine is to write a book about my life—my experiences as a child, a daughter, a wife, a mother, a nurse, and now a grandmother.

The inception of this dream began several years ago. In fact, I said by age 53, I would write a book. I am now in my 60s. It's long overdue.

It is then apropos that I finally begin to actualize this book as I spend this last quarter of my life. I retired in December of 2016, four months after my Dad passed away. I decided to fully retire from my nursing career so that I may be able to spend more time with those I love—my Mom, especially. A part of me died when my Dad passed on and I cannot begin to count or quantify the immense regret I feel for taking for granted the TIME I could have spent with him.

There is not a day that passes that I don't talk to him in my thoughts. A life as full as his cannot just end here but must go on, not only in the memories of our minds and hearts but beyond this physical realm. I know that one day, I will see him again.

Chapter 1

Got a Dollar?

The Second Secret: Don't die with your music still in you.

Kahlil Gibran said, "When you are born, your work is placed in your heart."

Dr. Wayne Dyer
in *10 Secrets for Success and Inner Peace*

My Dad and me

"*G*ot a dollar?"

"A penny for your thoughts," some say, but I say, "A dollar for the story of your LIFE!" Oh, if only LIFE was as simple as that.

But life is complicated and worth so much more.

This is my story . . .

My cellphone stopped working one weekend in August 2016. Apparently, no one could get a hold of me. They figured that's just me. I don't always answer my calls. This was a Monday, a day of rest for me as I was scheduled to work a twelve-hour shift the following day. My youngest daughter, who lives less than two miles away, suddenly showed up at my doorstep and said with an urgent voice, "Mom, everyone's been trying to call you! Daddylu is not doing well. You better go and see him right now. Go as you are. They think he might not make it through tonight!"

"What? What are you talking about?" I said with the wheels turning inside my head and butterflies stirring in my stomach. But I pushed away any thoughts of impending doom that may begin spreading through the ether and affect the outcome even more. "Oh, no. No. This is not happening."

I visualized my Dad's face as I drove like a madwoman up north.

"No, Dad. No, Dad." My thoughts kept whispering in my head, while my eyes alertly scanned the freeway. I'll make it there. Please, GOD, keep me safe.

I made it there at lightning speed. My heart was pounding as I quickly walked to my parents' G-suite. G-suite is the name we gave our parents' extension to their home. It is a kind of mother-in-law apartment, which is connected by a short breezeway to the main house.

To my surprise, everyone was already there, including my husband standing at the foot of Dad's bed! How is that possible? He didn't even call me. Bill must have responded immediately and driven from his office, which is a lot farther from our home where I was coming from. How much he must love my Dad!

The family surrounding my Dad's bed filled the room to maximum capacity. My Dad was barely breathing. His eyes were closed, and his face was slightly pale. I approached his bedside quickly and, with a loud voice, said, "Dad! What are you doing? What's going on? Why are you doing this?"

My Dad, a man of great inner strength and mental capacity, opened his eyes and mumbled something in less than audible terms. Was it a groan? Then, he signaled for his writing pad and a pen. I turned to find these and gave them to him. Mustering his energy, he wrote, "Why is everyone gathering around me?"

When I read this, everyone lifted up their voices, relieved that Dad was responding. One particular voice stood out. It belonged to my niece, Candice. She said excitedly, "DADDYLO, BECAUSE WE LOVE YOU!"

With a weak voice, his quick response was, "Oh."

Then, the room filled with the joy of laughter, and great sighs of relief.

Deep inside my soul, I held my breath—believing and disbelieving, denying the stark truth that peeked in through the corners of my mind. Is denial the answer for a heart that cannot hold more pain? Or a mind that cannot possibly accept the inevitable? Is the inevitable (death) the enemy that lays crouched in the corner of one's mind ready to pounce and devour? Or is it a dark cloud that always somehow tries to move in and block the sunlight from the inner landscape of our hearts? Yes, it is. And the antidote to death and my fear of death that I have found through the years is FAITH in my GOD who loves with no end, who answers our prayers, and who can deliver.

Tonight, the GOD of LIFE answered my prayers, saw our tears, felt our pain, and He knew to grant and extend our Dad's life on this earth. Tonight, he did deliver!

In the U.S., there is a memorial service held in honor of the person who has passed away, which is referred to as a "Celebration of Life." This phrase is so hard for me to understand. For when death comes to someone close to me, it is without a doubt, a time of mourning, a time of pain, and a time of sorrow and extreme grief. It is not a time for celebration. Death is death, a cessation of life, a very tangible separation from one's loved one. Death is so tangibly and painfully final. To me, death is the enemy.

I know I should look upon death in a more enlightened way, but this is truly how I feel.

There was no question or doubt that I would not go to work the following day. I'm going to spend the night with my Mom and Dad, I said to myself. I called and spoke with my long-time friend and assistant nurse manager and explained. "Of course, Maribel," she said. "Stay with your Dad. Take as long and as many days as you need." These were the kindest words—she said exactly what I needed to hear. She, too, had lost her dad years ago, and she knew the value of a few "cents" left in one's life.

The night was rough for my Dad. It was now visible to me that he truly was very ill. He was not a complainer, you see. He always lifted up other peoples' spirits and never showed anything less than the strength of great character. Gregarious by nature, a public figure, a leader, the focal point of any gathering—he was a charismatic man with a heart of flesh.

In many ways, my Dad epitomized a man of strength, but at the same time, he was soft, a man of steel, yet not stiff and unyielding when it came to matters of the heart. This was my Dad. He believed in GOD. He was spiritual, but not a religious fanatic.

He was a man of science with the wisdom of a healer. This was my Dad, my hero. He was 84 years old, and it had been nine and a half years since his initial diagnosis of cancer. He had had three surgeries, but never chemotherapy. He opted for the natural boosting and healing power of the body and used megavitamins in his IVs, a process called IV Nutritional Therapy.

With the shock of his initial cancer diagnosis, he changed his entire lifestyle. He read avidly (which he had always done) all materials and periodicals about alternative medical research pertaining to cancer and the ways to avert its destructive course. Chemotherapy destroys both normal and cancerous cells. It has no regard for specifics once it is integrated into the body. With this in mind, my Dad and our whole family made a unanimous decision that chemo was not an option.

With the help of his brother, who is also a medical doctor, my Dad was able to arrange for IVNT (IV Nutritional Therapy) to be given to him at home. After the initial diagnosis, my sister and I, both nurses, took turns administering his IVs every day for the first two weeks, and then three times a week, tapering off the frequency down to once a week and then nothing for about three months.

My Dad was cancer-free for three to four years after that intensive treatment.

A change of lifestyle—i.e., a healthy diet, no alcohol, daily mild exercise, use of relaxation music to evoke a calming effect on his psyche, a return to GOD and having Faith in His great healing powers—I believe, played a role in my Dad's healing process.

In addition, Dad had the immense support of our Mom and our whole family as well as numerous friends—we all did everything we could to surround him with nothing but POSITIVE energy. Our answered PRAYERS for healing without a doubt played a big part in my Dad's remission.

Although remission can be partial or complete, we chose to believe and celebrate our Dad as "cancer-free." We were all so happy for him and life went on.

However, forgetfulness regarding one's demise and self-reliance versus GOD-dependence can bring us back to our old lifestyle choices. And like all humans, we all have our weaknesses and so we slide back to comfort, which later brings us much discomfort. And so, it was with my Dad. The uninvited visitor, which lay dormant for years, showed its ugly head once again in my Dad's body.

My Dad fought this enemy from mid-2006 to August 2016 until it found its way up higher and higher in his body, from his colon until it affected his most vital organs such as his liver and lungs. Throughout all this, my Dad never missed a beat. He lived his life to the fullest.

He enjoyed traveling throughout Europe and this country with my Mom and my sister, Tess, and her husband. Whenever Tess went to some nice place to travel for vacation, she would always take along my Mom and Dad. This allowed them to visit interesting places for the first time and to better enjoy their retirement years. I'm very grateful to my sister for doing that for them. She truly made her time count with our parents.

Then, finally toward the very end, my Dad's heart was set on returning to where he began his journey in this lifetime, where he was born in our little town in the Philippines. Where the seed was planted, raised, and grew, this tree (my Dad) wanted to be re-planted for a time in its native ground.

So, he returned to the Philippines several times to continue his compassionate medical missions there, especially for the poor, the ones he loved the most and who loved him back for all he had done for them. Several of his colleagues volunteered their time to give free medical services to the poor in remote places once a year. My Dad was known for his heart of gold. My Dad's final visit to the Philippines was a few months before he passed away.

That Monday night in August 2016, my husband and I slept in my parents' G-suite, my husband on the couch and me between my Mom and Dad with our heads on opposite ends of the bed.

The night was rough for my Dad. He was up several times to go to the bathroom and after several trips, exhausted and short of breath, he sat on the very edge of his bed with his arms draped over the backside of a chair, his shoulders hunched. His elbows and arms hung down in a resting position, to expand his "wing and wind" capacity, thereby, naturally aiding his breathing.

His condition was tricky because the more short of breath he was, the more anxious he became, which in turn made him even more short of breath. A very small dose of anti-anxiety medication was given as needed. We were always careful not to give too much to avoid over-sedation, which would cause him to forget to breathe.

His breathing treatments helped with the ease of air exchange, but the side effects included increasing his heart rate. This was problematic because his heart rate was already elevated due to his anxiety from being short of breath. So, the breathing treatments were both helpful and adversive to my Dad's condition.

My Dad would nudge me gently with his hand whenever he needed something. He barely slept a wink that night. That was a long rough night for my Dad.

By morning, my Dad was totally exhausted. This was now Tuesday. The day he nearly died, and we called 911 because he kept rolling his eyes upward toward one side and he stopped breathing.

I remember holding my Dad's frail body in my arms like a little baby as I struggled to get him to sit up. Almost losing hope, I whispered into his ear, "Dad, Dad please don't . . .."

Someone said to call 911. Another voice said, "Begin CPR." I breathed into my Dad's mouth and instantly he responded. His frail chest moved as he heaved a big breath. I heard my Mom scream in the background, "Oh, no Abel! I'm not ready!"

Fear gripped her heart, panic and helplessness were apparent in her voice, but I told her firmly to please be quiet. My whole being was intensely focused on my Dad. I felt my spirit reaching out to his spirit, silently and urgently supplicating to the Great Spirit, the Great Giver of Life, to restore my Dad to life. Instantly, with one more big breath from me to him, my Dad revived and with a big gasp, he began breathing on his own.

The medics came in less than 10 minutes. We were so fortunate to have them just down the hill from my parents' home. The three men all moved efficiently with purpose and intent like ONE BODY—one gathered information, one administered oxygen, and another checked vitals and blood oxygen saturation to assess my Dad's condition.

My Dad was on continuous oxygen via a nasal cannula with the oxygen tubing connected to a large oxygen tank on the opposite side of the room. The tubing was buried underneath his bed covers. The tubing connected him to continuous oxygen except during the time he received his breathing treatments. He had several breathing treatments throughout the night that involved a bronchodilator to treat or prevent bronchospasms and to make breathing easier. Because he was hypercapneic (meaning that he was a CO_2 retainer), due to COPD (chronic obstructive pulmonary disease or chronic breathing problems), it was imperative that air, not oxygen, was used for his breathing treatments because high oxygen delivery would nullify his respiratory drive. To further explain, for a person with COPD, a low amount of oxygen drives the need to breathe because the body gets used to the high levels of CO2; in a healthy person, it is high levels of carbon dioxide in the blood that drive the need to breathe.

By morning, this tube exchange was overlooked as an issue. Because my Dad was up and down to the bathroom throughout the night, he ended up being on room air instead of continuous oxygen. As soon as the medics blasted him with 100% oxygen via a facemask, his oxygen saturation shot all the way to 100%. My Dad opened his eyes briefly and his color came back immediately. My Dad's fast recovery was nothing short of a miracle! He was taken by ambulance to Evergreen Medical Center in Kirkland. Immediately following his successful recovery of breathing (no chest compression was even needed), the lead medic asked immediate family members for relevant information regarding my Dad's health history. No, he wasn't in hospice; yes, the cancer was stage IV; and yes, he was a doctor.

Several of our family members are in the medical field so the medic felt that we were all "in the know" regarding our Dad's condition (i.e., his diagnosis, medical history, medications, and treatment options). The head medic said, "It sounds like there's enough medical knowledge and expertise here. So, we will proceed to take him to the hospital now that he's fully recovered with his oxygen saturation at 100% and since his vital signs are stable." As soon as this medic said this, I was struck with this thought: The littleness and nothingness of man and the greatness of GOD. We felt humbled and relieved due to my Dad's fast recovery after such a scary ordeal.

With this realization, I was painfully aware of the fact that it doesn't really matter how much we know or who we are, when life is nearly snatched out of our hands, we realize:

We are nothing. We know nothing. Only GOD has the power to restore and give LIFE.

✷ ✷ ✷

Everyone in the family, from children to grownup grandchildren, was notified of Dad's condition, and all came to gather at the emergency department visitors' lounge at Evergreen Medical Center. They were called from wherever they were, at home or work. They dropped everything and left to go to the hospital to see our Dad.

My uncle, my Dad's younger brother, Azael, and our youngest brother, Bong, flew in from Florida and Virginia, respectively, and arrived in Seattle shortly after they were notified of Dad's emergency situation. They were both able to see him while he was still in the emergency department.

Unable to talk, Dad was holding his thumbs up and smiling at those who came to see him.

Our youngest brother, the tenth of ten children, said this with an ear-to-ear smile, "Dad, you're a winner. You're really something else, Dad! You're incredible! Love you!"

In the emergency department, a new chest tube was inserted, and my Dad was kept on 100% oxygen by face mask and hooked up to all necessary monitoring devices. My Dad looked relaxed despite the trauma of a near-death experience he had just had a few hours ago.

Surrounded by all his loved ones, Dad was now resting quietly and peacefully awaiting transfer to his inpatient (intensive care unit) room.

Chapter 2

Death Comes to Us

In this stream, there is no seam between life and death.

Kathleen Dean Moore
in *Wild Comfort: The Solace of Nature*

*M*y Dad was admitted to the critical care unit or CCU on a Tuesday. This was Day 1 of his hospital stay. He was on 100% oxygen via face mask and all monitoring devices were in place. He had received a new chest tube to replace the old one he had from his previous hospitalization the week prior to this.

The attending doctor wanted to put an ET (endotracheal) tube in place as soon as my Dad was brought to his CCU room and admitted, but my Dad declined as he felt he would not be able to tolerate the procedure. We, his family, also felt this was unnecessary as his vital signs were now stable and his oxygen saturation levels were great, and, at this point, he was comfortable and breathing on his own.

My Dad rested during the night. My Mom and I stayed with him and spent the night at his bedside. This was Tuesday evening. He did well.

By morning, now Wednesday, the medical ICU team rounded on my Dad while he was fully awake. Because his throat was hoarse, he was communicating primarily through writing. He had been communicating in this manner for the past week.

Up to that point, being the man that he was and with his great medical knowledge, he was orchestrating his treatment plan.

This is a sore subject for me. I felt strongly that the attending physician had already formulated her prognosis of my Dad even before seeing him. During this first morning of medical rounds with my Dad present and fully awake, this same doctor said to us, his family, "OH, HE'S GOING TO DIE!"

In response to this, my Dad wrote on his writing pad, "GIVE ME A CHANCE TO LIVE!"

To this day, I have kept this tablet with all his handwritten statements and requests. Needless to say, I was not too happy with that doctor. She may have rank, knowledge, and experience, but she certainly did not show the least bit of compassion or kindness toward someone who could definitely have used it.

I stood by my Dad's bedside, holding his hand and trying to comfort him in the face of this very emotionally unsupportive, or detached, doctor who had just bluntly told him that he was going to die. I was furious and shocked at her bedside manner. Here is a sick man, a very sick patient of hers, who was on the precipice of death. He didn't need to be bluntly reminded of that!

My Dad squeezed my hand from time to time prompting me to just listen to the doctors and not get upset. But it was hard to suppress my emotions as I was reading to the team of doctors whatever my Dad wrote on his writing tablet. I was the one who read: "GIVE ME A CHANCE TO LIVE!" I was livid and trying to control tears of sadness and anger—sadness for my Dad and anger toward this calloused and insensitive doctor. "How dare she!" I thought.

Dad was on respiratory isolation for a presumptive pulmonary or lung infection. Analysis of his sputum was obtained without the need of an endotracheal tube insertion as was previously ordered by his attending doctor. He was also NPO (or "nothing by mouth") to prevent possible aspiration. This meant he was not allowed to have anything to eat or drink orally.

Parched for fluids due to this NPO status and the high oxygen delivery, my Dad requested some Jell-O and that his oral cancer medication be picked up from home. The doctors declined this first request, holding fast to their order of "nothing by mouth" to prevent risk of aspiration. A feeding tube was ordered to be inserted whereby he could have medications and nutrient-rich tube feeding could be started to provide means of cellular nutrition without him having to swallow and thereby increase his aspiration risk.

Dad asked for an oncology consultation right away regarding his oral chemotherapy drug, Tarceva, which he had started taking prior to being hospitalized. He had had two out of four doses so far.

The heme-oncology doctor lauded the positive results of Tarceva for how it had helped the majority of his patients. Encouraged by this positive report, my Dad insisted on resuming taking this oral chemotherapy drug especially since he only had two doses left of the total four prescribed. He took his third dose Tuesday night, the day he was admitted. The following day, Wednesday, Dad took the fourth, or last, dose of this chemotherapy drug.

As per hospital protocol especially with someone with a pulmonary issue, Dad had another chest X-ray on Thursday morning. The X-ray showed a dramatic change in his lungs. They found a powdery-like substance, which gave a hazy appearance to his good lung. The alarming part of this finding was that this was a new development. It wasn't there before on admission or on his baseline chest X-ray. I remember the doctors asking me how the IV Nutritional Treatment Dad was receiving at home was prepared. They wondered if we had to reconstitute the vitamin supplements added into the IV fluids from a powder. No, I told them, everything came in solution form in vials, which consisted of mega doses of vitamin C and all the essential vitamins and minerals.

In looking back, the doctors never mentioned anything about the oral chemotherapy drug Tarceva's side effects, which include causing interstitial lung disease and possibly death. Because we trusted our Dad and his ultimate decision to take this oral chemotherapy drug for an extremely short period of time (once daily for four days), we didn't bother to read about it or question how much of a risk he was taking. And he finished all four doses; two were taken at home before he went to the hospital on that fateful Tuesday morning and two were taken during his hospital stay and before his chest X-ray Thursday morning.

On Thursday, his change of status was noticeable. His breathing and level of comfort had taken a turn for the worse. Everything continued to go downhill on Thursday night.

Adding to Dad's decline, he had been without food or nourishment for those first three days (Tuesday, Wednesday, and Thursday). And the feeding tube in place never reached a maximum level or rate for his ailing body to receive adequate cellular nourishment. So, his body was compromised by malnutrition and dehydration, making it ever more difficult to fight cancer!

At this point, I realized that Dad's condition was getting worse. His breathing and his pain became the focal point in his fight for life.

Each night during his hospital stay, I spent the night and went home briefly to shower and change, but I always returned to my Dad's bedside to be with him every sleeping and waking moment that I could.

My brother, Gerry; sister, Seset; niece, Candice; Cheisi (my nephew's wife); and niece, Cristalle, all took turns staying up with him, writing down his vital signs and O2 sats or oxygen saturation, and making sure he was comfortable.

My uncle Tito Nene (Dr. Azael Borromeo), who flew in from Florida on Tuesday, the day my Dad was admitted to the hospital, came to visit my Dad every day as well.

On Friday, my uncle said his goodbyes to my Dad and flew back to Florida the following morning. I remember him saying on this last visit, "Boy! You guys are tough." I didn't really understand what he meant then. But, looking back now, I realize where his heart was coming from. He was wondering how we could stand to see our Dad, his brother, suffer as he did. As for me, I saw that

Dad was uncomfortable, but I looked at him and his condition as part of the process of his illness. I expected that recovery was coming and that he would pull through this as he had done in the past. I believed that he would get well and then be discharged and return home. It was just going to take a while. I never gave up hope. I never entertained any thought that would suggest otherwise. Death was not an option despite the grim prognosis of his doctors.

Friday night, the fourth night, was a really rough one for Dad. He was conscious but I now noticed that he was unable to move his right hand. He must have had a stroke that night. His breathing was more labored although his oxygen saturation readings were high due to having continuous oxygen at 100% via a face mask. My Dad was in a bad place. He no longer opened his eyes to see who was around like he usually did on previous nights.

The following day, a new set of ICU doctors rounded on him and called for a family conference outside of my Dad's room. This was in the lounge that was reserved for us and where some of our family members slept overnight during Dad's entire hospital stay.

Present at this family meeting were my Mom; me; my brother, Gerry; and my sisters Marilyn, Tess, and Seset. These ICU doctors were very calm and asked us if we had any questions or concerns. Then, they told us Dad's lab results were not good, although his vital signs and oxygen saturation readings were within the normal range. They also explained that his lactic acid levels were very high indicating a shift of the acid-base balance in his body chemistry. With my pre-knowledge of these things, I knew this was not good news! Although this information may sound benign to people who do not understand these critical acid-base balance shifts, it is a matter of life or death if not corrected. The doctors shifted their focus for Dad's treatment to "comfort care." They explained that they didn't want Dad to be uncomfortable and have a hard time with his breathing. They prescribed intravenous morphine as needed to alleviate his pain and labored breathing. In addition, they continued his Albuterol nebulizer treatments routinely and as needed. Morphine helped his pain but, of course, made him too lethargic resulting in his mental status starting to decline—narcotic-induced lethargy is a morphine side effect. In the first initial days of hospitalization, Dad was awake a lot and able to get out of bed to use the urinal. By his fourth day, he was too tired, lethargic, and it took too much out of him to do this, so they placed an indwelling Foley catheter in him, which also helped in monitoring his fluid intake and urine output more accurately.

Saturday came around and my Mom announced to us that she would stay in the hospital overnight. So, I drove her to pick up some clothes and necessities from her home and then back to the hospital. Their G-suite had been totally rearranged. A hospital bed was placed in the middle of their living room to allow for space and ease of mobility when Dad would eventually come home from the hospital. So, we were very hopeful—never did HOPE leave our hearts. Dad was going to come home!

Meanwhile, the family planned to have their church service in the hospital chapel that following day, which was Sunday morning. I went home and changed.

When I came back to the hospital, my Dad took a turn for the worse. I was greeted by his RN who said he wasn't doing well at all. My sister, Tess, was beside herself with panic. Everyone was called to see him as the nurse had informed us that he may not make it through this day. This was Sunday afternoon, August 21, 2016. When I returned, the scene at the hospital was alarming to me. Those inside my Dad's room stood surrounding his hospital bed. Why are all these people here? My head was reeling.

The room quickly filled to full capacity—with some standing outside, looking through the room's large glass wall hoping to have a glimpse of our Dad, who was NOW in his last breathing moments. It was obvious that Dad was in agonal breathing—the kind of labored breathing that precedes eventual death. Everyone was watching and praying, some had tears, and not one soul was without grief written all over their faces.

We all witnessed him take his last breath. For me and my family, this was the day the moon left, and the sun refused to shine!

I didn't know how to act, how to feel, how to continue to live without the man, my earthly father, who knew my heart so well and always had room for me in his.

Dad's last breath was loud and distinctly pronounced—the sound was as if a jet was being launched!

He tried. He really tried to hang on to this life. He wasn't ready to leave us behind. He wasn't ready to go just yet. But his lungs failed, his heart failed, and his body could no longer fight the inevitable.

Death does come to us, unwanted though it may be. This event will take a while for me to digest and swallow emotionally. The grieving process begins . . .

Chapter 3

Retracing My Footsteps

Part 1

Childhood Memories

I grew up in the Philippines in a small town on an island off Cebu Province. The third of 10 children, I lived a sheltered but privileged life. My Mom was busy popping out children left and right while my Dad was in medical school. So, from age two to five, I lived with my maternal grandmother. At such an early age, I naturally attached to my Grandma, as if she were my mother, since she became my primary caretaker. By the time I entered first grade, my Dad had become a full-fledged MD and had his own clinic, following in his own father's footsteps.

This was a difficult period of transition for me because, by then, I was used to being the only small child in my maternal grandmother's household, which consisted of four generations of adults: my grandmother's parents (Lolo Lucio and Lola Inez) and her grandmother (Nanay Heronima) and my Mom's brother (Tio Max). I was the center of attention.

When my Dad established his clinic, he was adamant about bringing all his children together under one roof. I recall one particular incident when I saw my parents' maid coming toward my Grandma's house while I was looking out the window. I knew what was happening because this was obviously not the first time they had sent someone to come get me. Panicked, I started scratching my hands, arms, and face to feign a measles rash. I told my Grandma, "Please don't let them take me away, Mama. Tell them I'm sick with the measles!"

My Grandma obliged as I clung to her skirt for dear life. The maid was sent away. I can't recall exactly how I finally came to live with my parents and siblings permanently. They must have tricked me somehow, but I do remember crying and crying for my Grandma every night from missing her so darn much.

It was a traumatic period of separation and adjustment. I eventually did adjust but was constantly picked on by my older two siblings for being such a crybaby. At this early age, I knew the trauma of separation, of feeling like an outsider, of feeling alone and not accepted, and of being uprooted from the surroundings I had gotten used to. When I finally came to live with my parents at their house, I felt more comfortable sitting on the lap of one of our maids and preferred to eat with them in the kitchen rather than in our dining room sitting with my siblings.

The maids were fun and simple people. They told a lot of stories. Their food was not like my family's food; it was plain but, to me, very tasty. They ate with their bare hands, so I learned to eat like them without utensils.

After dinner, my parents would have us all line up in front of them to do some "program" or performance. I'd sit on my Dad's lap instead. There, I felt safe, I felt loved, and I felt secure. My Dad never held back any reservations about telling everyone I was his "favorite," whether it was in front of family or his friends.

And this, to everyone's knowledge, went on throughout my older years. Everyone accepted the fact that I was my Dad's favorite child even into my old age!

During the program or performance, our parents would ask us one by one what we wanted to be when we grew up. When it was my turn, I'd say proudly "labandera" meaning "laundry woman"! They would all laugh, amused at my great ambition.

In my country, the Philippines, it wasn't uncommon to have several household helpers. Each one had a specific assignment or duty throughout their day. The laundry woman fascinated me the most with her "antics" I called them. She would soak the dirty clothes in one big bucket and pull them out one by one. Each item would be stretched out and rubbed with a bar of soap all over. The clothes would be rubbed on themselves vigorously to remove the dirt. Then, they were squeezed, rinsed, stretched up in the air, and beaten with a flat wooden paddle. Next, the clothes were twisted, rinsed again, and wrung out. This process was repeated until all the suds were gone and the water was clear.

To me, as a child observing all this was like watching a dance of sorts—some form of art, a skill requiring patience, determination, and strength. For me, it was beautiful and fascinating to watch.

The laundry woman had some type of blue liquid she added to bring out the brightness on all the dingy whites. After she was finished with all the laborious washing, she would then hang all the clothes on a clothesline. The climate in the Philippines is perfect for drying things naturally with sun and air! There was no such thing as a washing machine or clothes dryer. When the laundry woman was done with this task of hanging the clothes, she would take a break for lunch.

After lunch, we would take our short afternoon nap ("siesta" time), then be woken up for our afternoon merienda (snack) of boiled sweet potatoes (camote) or fried sweet plantains with cocoa or chocolate swirl muffins. At this time, the laundry woman would set up for ironing the clothes, which took up all afternoon until about 5 or 6 p.m.

The ironing too required special skills—making perfect pleats for skirts or ironing seams on pants or making stiff collars for shirts. To heat the heavy-duty, black, cast-iron iron, the laundry woman placed red hot charcoals through an opening in the top using tongs. When the iron was hot enough, she would begin to press the clothes. The iron would stay hot for the day, maybe there would be a change of hot charcoals once or twice. She used a dampened cloth or lightly sprinkled water to wet each item to be ironed. By 6 p.m., she was completely done with her tasks and joined the rest of the helpers for supper. All this in a day's work! Her hard-working hands were gnarled and adorned with prominent veins on the surfaces, branching out like a frond of seaweed—the mark of a hard-working woman.

I admired her skills. Thus, it was my ambition to be like her when I grew up!

At night, the helpers would listen to a nightly drama on a small transistor radio. There was no TV then. Everyone was quiet and closely followed with their ears as their eyes were fixed on the radio. They seemed to be watching the stories unfold, their imaginations on high alert to all the little nuances and sounds. It's amazing how much the ears can transmit and translate those sounds into nothing less than vivid visions—it was as if they were watching the drama on a big screen TV!

One of my favorite childhood comfort-evoking memories is waking up to my Grandma's slow stirring of her sikwate, a hot chocolate drink made from bitter organic chocolates, which came in round tablets called "Tablia." She preferred her drink thick and strong. The slow rhythmic stirring was magical. She once gave me a taste, but to my young sweet tooth, it wasn't as sweet as it sounded while she was stirring it, nor did it come close to being as sweet as its sweet aromatic smell!

When we moved to this country, my Mom would make us hot cocoa in the mornings. Then, decades later, when Starbucks first came around and espresso stands made their appearance, I found my favorite hot drink—to this day, I am addicted to mocha. This comes closest to the sweet memories embedded perhaps in my subconscious from my Grandma drinking sikwate. Such nostalgia!

The taste of mocha brings me comfort, and its sweetness brings back nostalgic memories of my Grandma, my Mama Aning, and her daily morning drink. Mocha for me in these modern times and Mama Aning's sikwate in her time.

At my Mama Aning's house, I have sweet recollections of our evenings together. After dinner, this little family of my Grandma's multi-generational household would go out on the front porch and sit gazing at the stars while blowing their tobaccos. Cigar and cigarette smoke rose into the cool balmy air. My great grandfather smoked a pipe called a cuaco; my great grandmother smoked cigars; and my grandmother smoked teeny, skinny white cigarettes (the brand name was "SPORTS"). I sat on my Grandma's lap counting as many stars as I could see and feeling comforted as she rocked her rocking chair slowly. Everyone was quiet—engulfed in this scenery, alone with their thoughts, but breathing the same air and being of one heart; there was no question about that. I was content and happy. I have such fond memories of this time of my life.

Growing up in that little town at that particular time in life was very blessed. It has, of course, changed tremendously since those childhood years.

Our—my family's—house occupied a prominent corner lot in the middle of the town on a very visible and busy intersection. Our house stood immediately across from a seashore full of mangrove trees. The beach was not the kind we expect of a beach—white and sandy. It was instead where mangroves grew best; the beach was the dark muddy kind with soil soaking in seawater where hundreds of tiny burr holes housed multi-colored little crabs. At low tide these holes would open up and the little crabs would crawl out of hiding. These crabs were not for eating, but just there, I guess, to decorate the shore as Nature would have it.

As children, we would go down to that "forbidden" muddy shore and try to capture as many as we could of these brightly-colored little creatures called "agokoy." If you were not careful, these little crabs would literally bite off your fingers with their sharp little pincers. But their multi-colors were so irresistible—we could not help ourselves but go there and sneak out when we were supposed to be taking our afternoon naps.

The crabs were sunny yellow, bright orange, deep red, electric blue, sometimes purple, but mostly gray and black—these were the ones no one wanted to catch.

They came out when the tides were low and covered the blackness of the mud. As curious children, we snuck out and pursued these beautiful, enticing, pinching little sea creatures, put them in jars, and then emptied those jars on the sidewalk and made the crabs race or run amok. It was always fun and worth the risk. We would get into big trouble for this as our appearances betrayed where we had been. The distinct smell of seawater on our skin and the disgusting black mud caked in between our toes told on us. This always called for some maternal disciplinary action—the coconut broom whipping stick on our bare little legs. The maids got in trouble, too, for not doing a better job of watching us. We'd get a good scrubbing as my Mom was obsessed with having clean kids.

After that perilous and exciting adventure, and all somber from being apprehended, and crying, we fell asleep, attempting to resume our afternoon nap. Then we'd be woken up for our afternoon merienda. We would eat, all quiet and repentant, only to do it again months later! Those crabs!

Eventually, I learned to adapt to my new surroundings with my own immediate family: Dad, Mom, and siblings. Being busy having real life adventures was really quite fun. But at night, my mind took my heart by the hand and began to wander. There were tears on my pillow always . . . .

For years it was like this because I missed my Mama Aning so terribly.

We didn't have a lot of toys when I was growing up. Mostly, we used natural materials for toys and playthings—e.g., when we played "retail store," we would cut up leaves and flowers and cactus and put the pieces in jars, pretending they were food or ingredients like thick cooking oil, and we made mud pies as well. We used sticks as tongs and seashells were our spoons for scooping our pretend foods. We would make clicking sounds with our tongues and cheeks pretending to eat them. It would literally take us hours to play like this, stopping only to have meals with our family, then we would resume our play. Life was so fun and so wonderfully carefree then.

We also played running games, like who could outrun the rain coming from the hills down to the valleys (or town) before the eventual downpour reached us. I always thought I could outrun my three best friends—I could, but not without scraping my legs raw as I slid around corners, falling into a rough gravel ditch! Once, I was so scraped up that I got sick with a fever and my Mom wondered why I wasn't at the dinner table. Then, she found out what was wrong when she came to the girls' room. I had fallen asleep. I was so sore, I cried when she touched my scraped-up thigh. I still have traces of those deep scars caused by skidding around corners to win the race.

Looking back, we did have some "commercial toys," like a doll for each of the girls—nothing fancy or excessive as kids have today. We also played with jackstones, marbles, yo-yos, spinning tops, and hula hoops.

One particular incident, which I feel prompted to share, is this. One year, I had a Japanese doll with a pink silk long sleeve top and black silk pants. We were playing with our dolls that day and my older sister Marilyn played a trick on me. She wet the doll's pants and said: "Oh my gosh, your doll peed! You're going to be struck by lightning tonight because you will be baliwan." This meant that I would be punished for having this inanimate toy pee! Lo and behold, that night there was lightning and loud booming thunder that scared the wits out of us! It's true. OMG! I was terrified and hid myself in my closet.

My older sister knew I was very superstitious and gullible and so easy to scare. She enjoyed doing that to me. I was timid being the "newcomer" in my Mom and Dad's house because I had lived with my grandmother all those years before I joined them. Marilyn, my older sister, took advantage of my timidity and gullibility and played many tricks on me growing up! I was a crybaby and perhaps this really annoyed her. But that particular night, the lightning and booming thunder really scared her too! After that, I didn't play with that Japanese doll anymore. I think we threw it away.

More fun and exciting times in this little town . . .

Once a group of circus performers came to our town to exhibit their amazing talents. I remember their gravity-defying trapeze jumps, unbelievable body-twisting feats, and stunning out-of-this-world sequined costumes and beautifully made-up faces. We were so awestruck by these "ground stars." To me they were no less bright and amazing than the stars up in the sky—so I called them "ground stars." To us they were like movie stars or celebrities.

The drums and music for the performers filled the air with so much excitement. These people were unreal to us—amazing and truly out of this world. They came and they left and when they left, the circus's mesmerizing effect lingered for weeks in our quaint little town. We sang the songs they sang. We secretly wanted to be like them— beautiful, talented, and awe-inspiring "stars."

I remember us children trying to emulate their body-twisting feats like leaning all the way backward as if our spines were made of Jell-O. With our feet still firmly planted on the ground and our backs curved in a backbend, our heads upside down between our arms and legs and facing forward, we walked with our hands and feet like some configured human frogs or crabs!

I did it. We all did it. We children showed off and were proud that we could do their stunts, too, except of course for the trapeze number!

In the following months, early in the evenings after supper, we would look up at the stars in the sky and, as if daydreaming at night, those circus stars remained bright in our thoughts. Only this time, becoming a distant memory—but something one would never forget.

As Time is dynamic and therefore constantly changing, we too grew up. We were no longer little kids playing with mudpies and being chased by the rain.

The happy, carefree, ever-present-in-the-moment flow of a child's life gave way to daydreaming, secret crushes on full-grown adults, and staying longer in front of the mirror!

Spontaneity was exchanged for timidity and shyness. I could no longer sit on the pavement with my legs all over the place. My attention was called to this: I had to learn to sit like a little lady!

Part 2

Teenagehood

I left my childhood behind and transitioned into adolescence. But although I was transitioning into my adolescence physically, I was still the little girl at heart. Truly, a late bloomer!

I use the word "uprooted" as another term for transitioning. I didn't expect to be uprooted or moved out of my home again. The first time this happened to me was at such a tender age, between two and three years old when I moved from my primary home with my parents to my maternal grandma's, Mama Aning's, care. This I believe was very traumatic for me. I was fully aware of being separated from my mother, my first primary caretaker, and I didn't understand why it was happening. You obviously have no control or ability to fully express your pain and anxiety except to cry your head off and to annoy those around you even more. My Mom at that time was emotionally and physically overwhelmed and exhausted! She had two kids above me, one kid below me, and she was pregnant with the fifth child. I was taken in by my maternal grandmother (Mama Aning), kicking and screaming, I imagine. I don't remember this clearly, but most likely, this would have been the scene of such a parting of ways. Separation anxiety played havoc in my internal life for as long as I can remember. After living with my Mama Aning for a while, I got acclimated emotionally and psychologically to my new surroundings; her home was my safe and stable haven. Her patience won my love, and her love sustained me. She could not go anywhere without me right next to her. When we hopped onto a "jeepney," my Grandma would have to be assisted to get on it because she was old, but the porter would have to lift the two of us together because I would scream unless I was stuck to her waist. Both of us would get lifted up together! Looking back at this now, it seems so pathetic and ridiculous—but that's how it was. She tolerated my super clingy dependence on her.

Then, the second "uprooting" was when I was about five to five and a half years old. My Dad wanted to get his kids under one roof once he was able to start his own clinic and provide for all of us.

Again, this separation event, this time from my Mama Aning, caused me extreme anxiety and emotional trauma. I eventually got over it because Dad showed me so much love and attention, more than the other children, and I learned to feel safe and comforted in that new environment.

These were my public elementary school teachers in my little hometown of San Francisco, Camotes, in the Philippines. This school went from first to sixth grade:

1st grade: Nang Bebing

2nd grade: Nang Azun

3rd grade: Nang Pingping

4th grade: Nang Mameng

5th grade: Nang Agnes

It was customary for the girls in my family to be sent to an all-girls school after fifth grade. So, I was sent to the city to study at St. Theresa's College in Cebu City. This was an affluent or high-end Catholic school managed by Belgian nuns who were very strict and had high standards and expectations. English was the spoken vernacular in school. Being a newcomer in that school was a nerve-racking experience for me.

St. Theresa's College included the elementary grades as well as four high school grades. I went to school there from 6th grade through part of my senior year of high school. The boys in my family were sent to San Carlos.

During my fourth year of high school, I went partly to St. Theresa's and then to Queen Anne High School because we moved to the U.S. Interestingly, Queen Anne High School put me in the 12th grade as a senior. However, I did take a U.S. History class and a World History Class at the 11th grade level.

In the Philippines, in the public school system, there was no official preschool or kindergarten at the time and no middle school. Grade school tended to go from the 1st grade to the 6th grade. Then, there was high school: 1st year (freshmen), 2nd year (sophomore), 3rd year (junior), and 4th year (senior year). So, basically, in the Philippines, you received 10 years of education versus 12 years in the U.S.

In my hometown, the majority of my classmates dropped out of school after high school and the people from the mountains did even before that. Sixth grade was their full educational attainment, which became to them an accepted norm. They went on as their parents did, became adults at such a young age, married among each other, and carried on with their lives as their parents did before them. They became farmers, land caretakers, hired household help, or even fishermen.

Few went outside of their social niche. This I assume was the acceptable norm.

But for my family, higher education was not an option but an expectation. Careers were pre-chosen by our parents and schools/colleges were also predetermined.

"Tagabukid" literally means "from the mountains (bukid)." We children went to school with these children from the mountains as there was only one elementary school in our town. So, we intermingled with them in the school setting.

You could tell them apart from us because they had darker tanned skin and greasy hair that smelled like "lana" or coconut oil—something my Mom was not particularly fond of. The smell made her nauseous because it reminded her of copra (dried coconut)!

Also, these kids were timid and not socially inclined to mix with us. But they were really nice. I liked them and I particularly liked their lunch of pure cassava cooked in a round pot made of clay. No sugar was added to the dish. I liked the texture and the starchy, earthy taste of this ground root vegetable. I would exchange this lunch of theirs for a bale of lined paper, which they happily obliged. I did not have the moral understanding at the time to realize I was actually taking their only food for school that day.

My Dad was amused at me when he found out how much I liked their type of food.

Part 3

The Transition:
Childhood to Adolescence

I was sent off to the city to enroll in an all-girls Catholic school called St. Theresa's College, following in my older sister's footsteps. She lived in the city a few years before me with our paternal grandmother, and that was where I went to live as well. My path after the little town life was nerve-racking as I don't do very well with change. Homework was foreign to me because that was not something we did in my previous public school.

I now had to get used to having to live with new people again—at my paternal grandmother's house in Cebu City—and this was another difficult transition for me. When I talk about "uprooting," I mean the changes that come due to the transition to the next stage of life. Transition to adolescence for me felt like being uprooted from my familiar childhood.

I eventually met a couple of people or classmates with whom I felt comfortable, and I adjusted to my new life as a teenager, learning a new language (English), and a new lifestyle with new expectations. English was the only language spoken in the classroom. I struggled with that!

City living was totally different from what I was used to in my little town. It was busy, hectic, stressful, and lonely. Lonely because the lifestyle I was used to in my little town was simple and carefree.

My paternal grandmother was a lot different from Mama Aning (my mother's mom), who loved with no expectations. My paternal grandmother, Mama Dingding, was religious, very strict, regimented, and domineering. She was a real matriarch! I had to learn to live up to her expectations. But in her favor, I credit her for my great faith in GOD and in learning the habit of making prayer an important part of my daily life, albeit there was a lot of sense of duty and memorization and repetition of preset prayers versus understanding what we were praying about!

Our paternal grandmother's full name was Doña Celestina Parama Borromeo, known to us grandchildren as Mama Dingding. Doña is a title of respect used for a woman of a particular standing in society.

Although I found her to be harsh at times, I learned to look at her with new eyes. I learned that love isn't always being soft and easy going, that discipline is part of life, that hardship is rewarded with great results—e.g., studying hard means you get good grades. Life took on a different twist now. Although my paternal grandmother was deeply religious, she was also extremely status oriented. She grew up that way and acted that way. She knew and rubbed elbows with prominent people in the community. When I look back now, there was a lot of paradox in her life, something we learned to accept because she was our elder and honoring and respecting elders was the way to be. In contrast, my Mama Aning was very humble and quiet. She went to church, but she was not overly religious. She flowed through you like a soft breeze. Mama Dingding was a whirlwind of energy, over religious and someone who kept you on your toes always.

Just as I was adapting to this new environment in my teenage years, another big change came to our family unexpectedly. Once again, I felt the tinge of anxiety from feeling "uprooted." We moved to this country, the U.S., in 1971, in the middle of my senior year at St. Theresa's College.

My parents came one year before all of us moved to Seattle. This by far was probably the most challenging transition for me. An uprooting from one's currently established safe place to a new, unfamiliar environment was definitely daunting. The language, the culture, and making new friends was exciting, but unnerving. I was 17 going on 18. I was still a child inside compared to a lot of people around me who were already dating at that age. We, the girls in the family, were not allowed to date for fear that we would get married early and not finish our education. Although it was unspoken, it was understood as our family standard. Of course, it was different for our brothers—there was definitely an accepted double-standard. The girls were watched like precious jewels.

Our family moved to the U.S. for political reasons. There was a lot of political unrest in the Philippines in the latter part of the 1960s under President Marcos.

Since two of my Dad's younger brothers were already in the United States, my parents decided our family would follow suit for a safer and better future for us children and our family. This move was immediately prior to the advent of martial law in the Philippines.

My Dad's younger brothers were already well established here in the U.S.; one was a civil engineer who worked at Boeing and the other uncle worked as an MD in Ohio. My parents chose to live in the NW-Seattle area where eventually all our family members came to live and established it as our home base.

Our first home was in uptown Queen Anne, a perfect location because it was strategically located within walking distance of three schools that all of us children would attend. Our home was on 2nd West McGraw, only two blocks from McClure Middle School, a few blocks from Coe Elementary, and a mile and a half from Queen Anne High School where my brother (Abel Jr.) and I attended as a junior and senior, respectively. For me, walking that far especially very early in the cold and dark mornings was something I totally abhorred.

After I graduated from Queen Anne High School, I applied to the University of Washington Bachelor of Science in Nursing Program. Excited, I was ready to bury my head in the books and happy for my parents that they could have their dream and mine of becoming a Nurse. However, as life's twists and turns would have it, an unexpected bump on the road came when something more compelling derailed my plans from the path of self pursuit (the nursing profession) toward something higher and of more eternal value—the path of a missionary. I was just shy of graduating with a BSN/RN degree when I joined a controversial church and decided to follow my heart and pursue my own spiritual journey.

Part 4

The Detour

J joined an Eastern-based religious organization called the UNIFICATION Church, which taught basic principles that claimed would be the key to UNIFYING the WORLD through ONE FAMILY. I was with them for nearly three years and traveled the U.S. I spent about six months in upstate New York and six months in New York City in Manhattan, the Bronx, and Brooklyn. I got to travel and stay in other states, such as Maryland, Virginia, Massachusetts, Vermont, and Kentucky. I was assigned to Las Vegas and Lake Tahoe as my specific areas for missionary work. Later on, I traveled to California, Maryland, Massachusetts, Vermont, and New York. I also traveled to Washington, D.C.

In all these places, I got to meet people as a missionary. I learned a tremendous amount about individuals from all walks of life. This experience truly opened my eyes to a world way beyond the little bubble that I was raised in. It made me really seek GOD on a deeper, vaster level, and a more personal level than I was taught and brought up to do. It made me appreciate others—it made me more compassionate and more well-rounded. When we encounter people on our travels, we discover that all of us are the same regardless of race, origin, background, educational attainment, or social standing.

As a missionary, I found in my travels and in meeting people from all walks of life that the "real voyage of discovery" consists not necessarily in seeking new landscapes but in HAVING NEW EYES. I saw the world and people with a whole new perspective. I no longer pegged others based on their social standing or accomplishments. I looked at every person the same. I learned to love and appreciate people for who they are.

Our purpose in life is to be HAPPY. We all have hopes and dreams. Our beliefs and ways of living differ from each other, but we are all seeking the same basic needs with the ultimate purpose to be happy, regardless of race, culture, position, or possessions. Everyone desires the same essential things: love, acceptance, and to be valued.

I eventually left that church organization to return to my roots— my own family—and to pick up where I left off with my nursing career, believing that I could reach and affect more people in a positive, compassionate, and respectable profession like Nursing.

In my time traveling with this religious group, I had grown and matured in my ways of thinking. I was no longer afraid of change. I moved back purposefully on my own volition to revisit and resume my nursing education where I left off. This was also a dream come true for my parents. I'm grateful for my parents' wisdom and for GOD who watched over me, protecting and guiding my ways on a journey that eventually brought me back home safely, matured and intact. This return home and my decision to complete my nursing education was a long overdue answer to my parents' prayers!

As I write this book, I am learning about myself by retracing my footsteps from my childhood to now. The insights I've gained from these memories have taught me much about life as well.

Facing life's challenges through "transitions"—whether they be a change of environment or altered family relationships, a detour I didn't expect, etc.—though difficult, these events propelled me on to the next stages of my life. These allowed me to grow and develop my character to be who I am today. I am more inclusive of all people and more accepting of life and its necessary changes. My experiences have broadened my view of the world, strengthened my character, and softened some fixed ideas about people. The only challenge I find difficult to embrace is Death because to me, despite my faith and belief in GOD and in an Afterlife, IT seems so final—a truly painful goodbye—something I still struggle to embrace as reality and part of life itself.

Chapter 4

Serendipity

*An invisible thread connects those who are destined to meet,
regardless of time, place, or circumstance. The thread may stretch or
tangle. But it will never break.*

Ancient Chinese Proverb quoted in the book
An Invisible Thread by Laura Schroff

Part 1

Meeting Bill

$\mathcal{I}$love this "invisible thread" quotation (from some anonymous writer) because truly it was when my husband and I met that life began on a distinctly different level for me. I truly believe there are no coincidences . . .

Exactly nine years after our family moved to this country, I met my "husband-to-be" in the most serendipitous way. My family came to the U.S. in 1971, and I met Bill in November 1980. I was not introduced to him among friends or associates, at a party or any gathering, in a garden or a bar, on a dance floor, or in school or on a blind date. I was in between quarters nearing the end of nursing school; in fact, I was one quarter short of graduation.

During my time off from school, I felt an urge to do something different. I needed a fresh look at life outside of what I had grown accustomed to. I decided to volunteer at the Republican head-quarters and be part of the campaign for Ronald Reagan the first time he ran for president. Always a conservative at heart, but a rebel in my causes and my own choices, I felt this was the agenda for me at the moment.

It was one of those autumn days where everything just seemed magically beautiful. Actually, it was more like a spring day just adorned in different colors—autumn colors—with the air cool and crisp and without any of the Seattle rain!

Explore downtown Seattle. This was an urge rather than a voice inside my head that propelled me to go at that very moment. There was no internal dialogue or planning—just a spontaneous act. This is so "like me" to be led by life's Big Hand and go where my feet lead. And since my volunteer job did not require me to show up at any given time, spending my time exploring before heading to the headquarters was perfectly doable.

Additionally, at this time in Seattle in the 1980s, there was something called the "Magic Carpet" in a designated area in downtown Seattle. You could ride the bus in this zone for free. It was a program put in place by the city and King County Metro Transit to encourage foot traffic for the retail businesses.

I had lived in Seattle long enough to have seen the places downtown, but I lived in a "cultural bubble" related to my family's jaunts. Downtown Seattle was not a place I knew. When I got there that day, to my amazement, downtown Seattle's 1st Avenue all the way to the foothills of Queen Anne Hill, where my family first settled when we came to this country, was lined with many interesting historic spots. Before this day, I only knew Seattle Center and once visited with my family the magnificent iconic landmark of the Pacific Northwest, the Space Needle. But today was definitely different. I felt like I was setting my foot on important ground and seeing sites full of historical meaning. I felt adventurous, and carefree. I found myself in one of those old historic buildings admiring the intricately sculpted ceilings, observing the people around me, busily walking fast and past each other—too engrossed in their own busy world to enjoy their immediate surroundings. I smiled musing at this scene.

I was leaving the building when two attractive, well-dressed young men walked in briskly in stride with smiles and one of them in particular looked at me directly—I smiled back as I proceeded to go out of the building. I was looking up at the Free Bus Zone schedule outside when, to my surprise, one of those gentlemen I passed near the entrance was standing right behind me. I looked toward him and up to take in his towering, 6-foot-tall, well-built body, and sun-drenched, blondish red hair and mustache! His eyes twinkled as he spoke to me: "Do you work here?"

"No," I said smiling back, then quickly asked if he knew which bus to take to go to Virginia Street where the Republican headquarters was located. He didn't know. Without taking his eyes off mine, he wasted no time and asked if I wanted to go out to lunch with him. A little embarrassed, unsure of myself, and surprised, I skimmed my eyes around to quickly see if he was addressing me or someone else behind me.

Half-nervous, I smiled again and said, "I don't even know your name!"

"I'm Bill," he said as he stuck out his hand to shake mine.

From every human being there rises a light that reaches straight to heaven, and when two souls that are destined to be together find each other, the streams of light flow together and a single brighter light goes forth from their united being.

Baal Shem Tov (a Jewish mystical rabbi,
founder of Hasidic Judaism)

My hand felt like a petal inside his big, glove-like hand. I had never been approached so directly like that. And I haven't since!

I thought to myself, isn't there usually some form of flirtation at first? Or preliminary courting words? Well, his eyes and his looks did it for me! His total directness and confidence, devoid of arrogance or conceitedness, were very disarming. I told him my name. Then, he asked for my phone number. Without hesitation, I gave it to him, and he wrote it down on a tiny piece of paper.

"I'll call you!" he said.

"OK," I replied.

This chance encounter was the best thing that happened to me that beautiful sunny autumn day in November of 1980. And that approach, which took me by surprise, was a key to my future. I have always been somewhat slow to discern someone's advances. Had Bill behaved differently and less directly, I might not have responded the way I did and that would have been where spontaneous serendipity would have ended. Bill would have gone on his way and I mine. But, as the stars in heaven would have it, the UNIVERSE aligned with our hearts and created circumstances for us to meet at this crucial Moment in TIME. This meeting was meant to be!

I looked forward to Bill's call, but when I did not hear from him for a few days, I had my doubts. Just as I was mentally ready to write off this pleasant, exciting encounter to experience, he called early one Friday morning before seven! My brother, Gerry, woke me up. "A call for you Maribel. He said it's Bill."

Bill asked me out to dinner that evening. I said, "Yes."

Part 2

The Elaborate Dates

*W*ith Bill, I was introduced to fine dining—dinner at its best.

Our first dinner date was at the Olympic Hotel, which is now known as the Fairmont Olympic Hotel. I remember him walking in in his brown and beige tweed suit jacket. He looked even more dashingly striking than when I first met him. Having never dined at an exclusive place like that, I didn't know what to order except for a Caesar salad and Perrier water to drink.

"Can I order for you?" he asked.

"Sure," I said. "That would be nice!"

I thought, "Yeah. I like a man who leads and takes charge—just like my Dad. I feel safe with men like that. Self-confident and devoid of arrogance. I like that." He ordered for me filet mignon medallions, some veggies, and mashed potatoes formed like a swan. I learned from Bill that the shape had been created using a pastry bag. Then, we had dessert and wine. Well, he had wine; I had my Perrier.

We talked about family—nothing too deep, just getting to know our backgrounds and interests. I don't remember asking him what he did for a living because it wasn't important to me. But I couldn't help but notice what a gentleman he was throughout our entire time together. We were two young people who shared a lot of the same visions. We were both interested in buying houses, fixing them up, and selling them for profit. We shared the dream of getting ahead in life and we liked what we saw in each other. Our commonality later bound us together.

Bill had met me after work and had parked his maroon Cadillac Eldorado with white leather interior on the hillside by an alley that led to the side entrance of the Olympic Hotel. We sat in his car and resumed the conversations we had started over dinner in order to get to know each other better. As we talked, he made an off-the-cuff side comment: "Oh my gosh, did you see that huge rat run across the alley?" I told him no. He continued, "It was as big as a cat and carrying a piece of corn in his mouth!" I laughed. I couldn't believe this well-dressed gentleman would say that! But I guess he was serious and so was the rat. It must have been on a mission as it went back and forth carrying more food in its mouth! With that wonderful view, we soon got out of there fast!

Soon Thanksgiving was around the corner, and I hadn't heard from Bill. Then, all of a sudden, the long-awaited call came in the middle of the week. He invited me to come see him on his birthday, which happened to fall on Thanksgiving of that year in 1980! I had a bit of a dilemma as it was my family duty to make the table decorations for the Thanksgiving feast and to make sure everything looked beautiful for our guests.

Meanwhile, his co-workers had a birthday bash for him at his work so he couldn't make it to our family gathering. I was disappointed, but I still made time for him after my family's feast. And

I brought him gifts, which were somewhat odd and different, he later told me, but truly touched him like no others in his past.

I gave him red and green towels, an iron, and a shirt. No one had ever done that for him. I waited outside his apartment. He was a bit late in coming and just as I was getting ready to drive off, lo and behold, there he was standing by the driver's side of my car looking more charming than ever!

We drove together around Lake Union, and he stopped to show me his 30-foot sailboat kept at the Goves Cove marina. He said he was selling it so he could get a little house.

A few weeks later, he showed me the house he had bought. It was a little fixer-upper in Beacon Hill. I remember feeling so sorry for him because I had never seen a house in such a dilapidated condition! I mean everything needed repair from outside-in, ceiling to floor, and even the steps leading to the front door were cockeyed. You had to be careful not to fall in a hole, especially if you were wearing high heels like I was.

My heart went out to him. Little did I know at the time that this young man I was dating was a visionary. He talked excitedly about his plans to transform the house as he walked over to one corner of the living room and reached up to peel away part of the ceiling that was hanging down. Oh my gosh! I didn't know whether to laugh or cry for him—my heart melted as I saw another layer of this man underneath his good looks and style.

Our second date was at the original El Gaucho restaurant on 7th Ave and Olive Way in downtown Seattle close to where the Paramount Theater is today. It was old and fancy and dimly lit—the décor was from the 1920s. Bill wanted me to try their famous

Huntz breakfast served late at night on a cart and prepared right in front of you. Candlelight accentuated this romantic setting, which included a violinist dressed in a tuxedo who stopped at each table to serenade the guests. Very impressive. I had never experienced that before. Bill later told me how he didn't like the violinist because he spent too much time at our table! The music was so whimsical and appealing to my soul, I couldn't help but pay 100% attention to the musician. Little did I know that Bill also didn't like the attention I gave the violinist!

Our third date was at the Hyatt House restaurant in South Seattle by the airport. He introduced me to bouillabaisse, a French seafood stew, which I thoroughly enjoyed. To this day, it is still one of my favorites to order whenever we go out to dinner.

Our fourth date was at The Red Cabbage restaurant near the (now torn down) viaduct in downtown Seattle. Here I got my first taste of French-American-style escargots served as an appetizer. In the Philippines, fresh seafood is a staple as is the rice that goes with it at every meal. So, for me, seeing these six little curled up snails smothered in herb butter served in a hot cast-iron skillet was kind of a surprise! I was expecting to have a huge bowl or hot pot served with the snails still inside their beautiful shells and cooked in seawater to preserve their flavor.

I had a lot to learn! In this case, since escargots are land snails, seawater isn't considered for cooking them in, I guess, just lots of butter. I learned to develop a taste for escargots, but nothing comes close in comparison to the wild natural taste of the fresh sea snails boiled to perfection that I remember eating in my childhood.

The more I got to know Bill at this early stage of our dating, the more I realized there were so many layers to this man. I learned that he studied at the Seattle Institute for Culinary Arts and worked his way up from dishwasher to garde manger (or pantry chef). In French, "garder" means "to keep." And, later on, he became a sous chef at high-end restaurants. These jobs explained his great knowledge of food and what to order in these fancy restaurants.

For example, he worked at the Fairmont Hotel in San Francisco as the Chef Garde Manger, creating exquisite hors d'oeuvres, canapes, and eye-popping food displays including ice carvings. He also learned to work with tallow and make pâtés. The tallow, like ice, can be carved into centerpieces and lasts much longer than ice. Goose liver pâté, also called foie gras, is my favorite. Several years later, we found this quaint little European restaurant on First Hill called The Geneva, which served pâté de foie gras that we both fell in love with. The chef-owner was from Switzerland and trained in Swiss cooking. Being a culinary chef was a daunting task requiring skill, artistic talents, and patience. Bill recalls someone once saying to him, "Everything good takes time." This was said to him years before I met him and while Bill himself was carefully and skillfully carving a huge fish out of a block of ice. I have photographs of his food displays and ice carvings.

Before Bill, I had no clue what "culinary" meant—I had no idea that "culinary arts" existed as a curriculum offered at the college level. I thought cooks were just gifted individuals who had a knack for cooking, similar to how a talented gardener would be described as having a "green thumb"!

My world consisted of medicine, nursing, and family. Somewhere there was always religion and politics. Bill's life interests were totally different, consisting of work and working out. He was religious about staying physically fit and going to the Eagles Boxing Club in downtown Seattle daily after work or running around Green Lake several times. He would drink a protein shake with a spoonful of Brewer's yeast. He drank beer but never before his fights. Once, I met him at the boxing club after he had sparred with the Irishman Tommy Howard and another famous boxing sparring partner named Santana. Bill came out with blood on his boxing shorts and said proudly of his bout with Santana, "I beat him, honey!"

He was so passionate about this man-to-man sport of boxing that he actually set his heart on going professional. He trained under a coach named Sarge Little, who had been professionally training boxers for years. But, in the boxing arena, there are favorites who are, from the start, groomed to go pro. Bill was a tough boxer with talent and fierceness, but there were "hungrier" fighters than him. Still, he said he learned a lot from Sarge.

Although we were different in many ways, Bill and I shared core values and beliefs (i.e., our faith in GOD, the importance of family, and our conservative political values). In these ways, we were the same and remain so today. These common qualities bond us deeply. Thus, I believe you can be so different from each other, but if your core values are the same, you will be with each other longer than most people—even, perhaps, forever.

When Bill and I saw each other on a more consistent basis, we became one in mind and heart and missed each other when we weren't together at the end of the day. With that closeness, he articulated his clear expectations to me. He stated: "Now that we are together, you better see ONLY me."

Of course! I expected nothing less. His words clarified what I felt for him too. I was sure at that point we were meant to be together forever. I was so grateful I found someone who shared my thoughts, feelings, and beliefs. One who echoed the longing in my heart.

Exclusivity. Monogamy. Faithfulness. No open relationships. This clarified and echoed what I believe to be right and true. That said, not having had a wide variety of relationship experiences prior to Bill, I was quite happy to hear Bill say that to me because I had had one other brief relationship with an unstable soul who told me: "In America, you have an open relationship even if you are boyfriend-and-girlfriend." My gut instinct said: No way. This made me feel not right, insecure, confused, and unhappy. I thought at that time I had much to learn about this culture. Fortunately, I met Bill not too long afterward. And the more I got to know Bill at this early stage of our dating, my affection for him grew deeper.

When Bill's friends caught word that he got married, they couldn't believe it.

"No way, Wild Bill? The Barbarian?"

We had a very simple wedding ceremony attended by only a handful of people.

What they didn't know about Bill, but what I was privy to, was that we were both committed to making a life with each other by holding on to our core values through thick and thin.

However, there was a quiet side of Bill that I wanted to know and understand. I'd watch him grow pensive and look sad. I wished that I could read his thoughts, but I neither probed nor prodded. He would share with me what was going through his mind when he was ready.

He was going through a lot then. He wanted to enlist in the Navy to follow in the footsteps of his older brother, Harry. Harry had gotten married here in the U.S., joined the Navy, and moved to live overseas. When these events happened, Bill felt so alone and abandoned.

Every man has his own secret sorrows which the world knows not; and often times we call a man cold when he is only sad.

Henry Wadsworth Longfellow quotation by
President S. Monson during the Sacrament Meeting,
Sunday, August 19, 2012,
The Church of Jesus Christ of Latter-day Saints

At a young age, Bill's parents went through a bitter divorce and his brother was the only family he felt close to. Due to the divorce, Bill and his brother had to fend for themselves. While his brother attended high school, Bill worked. He was only 13 years old. Their plan was for Bill to support the two of them while his brother finished school and then his brother, in turn, would work to support Bill through school. But as fate would have it, this didn't happen once his brother joined the Navy and got married. The path his brother's life took, which sent him overseas, meant a broken promise to Bill.

When I met Bill, it was a sad, uncertain time for him and looking back made him pensive. But as the Great Hand of Fate would have it, I never would have met Bill if he hadn't gone off on his own and his brother hadn't left to make that possible.

Once his brother left to go overseas, Bill traveled across the United States hitchhiking, finding temporary jobs until he found some work he loved to do. There was no future stability at that period of time in his life. But being the fighter that he is and was, he never gave up. He kept himself busy with work and working out at the gym. He said he learned about work ethics from his father.

"The cream will rise to the top," his father used to say. He also instilled in Bill the desire to be the best he can be in whatever he does. "If you are a grave digger, be the best grave digger. If you are a dishwasher, be the best dishwasher." The bottom line was: "Work to support yourself and be the best you can be in whatever you do."

Despite the hardships he experienced (i.e., his broken family, working at a young age to support himself and his older brother, and his brother's broken promise to support him so he could finish his schooling), Bill kept going . . .

In addition to having dreams of being a professional boxer, Bill also dreamed of being a professional baseball player. He was a great pitcher in elementary school. He remembers his mom was always there for all his games. He loved the sport.

He is good at so many things. I have heard him say, "I could have been a great lawyer." That, too, was one of his aspirations. "But," he adds, "I never got the chance to finish school and go on to college because my parents got divorced." Broken dreams at an early age explained those deep pensive moments I noticed in him.

And these broken dreams crowded his mind as he lay in bed, alone in his thoughts. He would lie there staring at the bare light-bulb on the ceiling of his studio apartment, wondering about all the "if onlys." He continued to work and workout. These activities provided structure and inspired him to fulfill his many other unrealized ambitions.

Plan your work and work your plan.

Never give up. When you get knocked down, you get yourself up off the floor and keep going.

The cream will rise to the top.

These words played through his mind, like mantras.

Bill and Maribel
Hydroplane races in Detroit, Michigan, 2006
Beacon won the American Power Boat Association Gold Cup.

Bill has worked all his life from age 13 to now. He counts 140 jobs in his lifetime so far. Keeping track like this shows how important and embedded work life is in him. He has a chart of all the jobs he held from before I entered his life to now. The chart is framed and stands tall in our TV room. This huge, framed piece was given to Bill by our good friends Bill and Cheryl Osborne.

Telling Bill to retire or stop working so hard is like, in his own words, "trying to tell a racehorse in the heat of the race to stop running!" So, when people ask me if Bill will ever retire, I say to them: You have to ask him. I want him to, but he is his own man and will make that decision himself when he's ready.

So, as much as I would love for him to stop working so hard and assume a retiree's life of leisure and travel, my words fall on deaf ears as he chooses to do what he wants to do.

He now owns his successful business and feels much responsibility far beyond just taking care of our immediate family. For example, his business provides employment opportunities to both skilled and non-skilled workers. Through his business, community involvement, and hard work, he has helped so many people make a better life for themselves. And many more have benefited from his generosity.

This business started out in our home in Briarwood when our six children were in elementary school, middle school, and high school. The business tagline is familiar to people throughout the Pacific Northwest. He's the man behind the line: *Stop Freakin', Call Beacon!* He shares his story of starting his business with $6.00

in his pockets. This is true. His first toolbox was a drawer from our oldest son's dresser from when he was a baby. With rented tools and a small box truck, he went out daily to knock on doors and find opportunities to make money as a plumber. He once went to a gas station in Beacon Hill and offered to fix the leaky toilet for the owner-manager. He said he would do it for free. He also went to property management offices like Morris Piha Property Management and other places in the old Georgetown area where there are several industrial businesses and buildings and offered his work. He did all the work himself. He was fast and efficient. Soon, by word-of-mouth and by getting out there, Bill was never without a daily job. His customers loved his work and loved his personality and character. To this day, these people continue to be not only his customers, but friends for life.

Part 3

A Diamond in the Rough

*B*ill has fond memories of his childhood home in Mount Baker. Later in our life together, he would take me and the kids for a drive on his day off around the Lake Washington and Mount Baker area. He loved his family's old house on Hunter Boulevard, a three-story home occupying a large corner. He would point to the very top of the house and say, "That is my old room." I guess, like me, Bill loved revisiting his childhood memories too.

In the 60s, this home sold for 13K, in the 80s it went for about 800K, and in the 90s, it sold for about 2.4 million. Today, it is worth even more.

As a young couple with a big family, we could only share in his admiration for his childhood home and childhood recollections. We could never begin to afford such a house then. He showed us the "horse step" landing at the front on the pavement immediately in front of their home. This was for someone who needed to get off their horse-driven carriage. The person would step on the "horse step" before their foot hit the ground. Bill loves little details like this.

He has a couple of tender memories of his early childhood that he has shared with me. He had six stuffed animals, which he would tuck in before he went to bed himself. He had a pet dog named Rex that he would always feed first thing in the morning upon getting up and before he ate breakfast himself.

These traits are part of his core values. These traits have always been there and are still, to this day, very much a part of the man he is. He always puts others first.

We have six children who oftentimes would be asleep by the time he got home from work. He would find them in their bed and tuck them in with blankets and count them "like a hen gathering her chicks."

Sometimes, Bill puts others before his own family. This is a great trait to have, but his father used to tell him, seeing this nature in his son, "Son, don't bend over sideways to break your back." To this day, Bill is the same way and never quite heeded his father's words. Bill does things to the extreme and he's generous to a fault.

It has taken many years for me to fully appreciate this diamond in the rough. Over the years, I have tried to chip away at his many rough spots. He is tender yet he can be brash. He can be a teddy bear on the inside, but he is also at times an un-"bearable" taskmaster. People love him and perhaps hate him at the same time. There are many facets to this diamond. But the thing that outshines all his other personality traits is his charity. He loves to give, help, and serve. This is his language of love.

I found in my husband a strong man, a visionary man, a man wise and deepened in character through his difficult experiences in life. I found in him a heart of gold.

This is my love, my other and better half. He is my "diamond in the rough."

Part 4

A Poet

NOVEMBER 3, 2024

Quiet Time with Bill at the end of the day . . .
The businessman, the poet

*B*ill is a man of multi-talents. He has a way with words and is quite expressive and can be quite convincing to those who hear him speak. He is spontaneous and not afraid to speak from his heart. I am thus taken by his ability to express himself.

On one of our anniversary dinners at our favorite spot, Il Terrazzo Carmine, we talked about his oldest sister, Karen, whom he remembers fondly. She told him: "One day, you will meet a hippie girl, Billy." Then, Bill looked at me smiling—"I found my hippie girl—a flower child." With a blank look, I asked him, "Who?" With a laugh, he pointed to me and said, "That's you, honey!"

Bill went on and talked about how Karen bought him his first musical instrument, a violin. Karen was a first chair violinist in the Santa Barbara orchestra. He's proud of her accomplishments. "Too bad you never got to meet her," he continued. "She would have loved you." "Karen knew the right words to say to you," I replied. To this he responded, "No, she had the right HEART to give." These are words spoken by a wise old soul, I thought.

Bill, in our younger years, used to write me messages on pieces of paper. He would leave his messages where I could readily see them upon waking up. Here is one of my favorites. He wrote this in 1998—after we had been together for 18 years and had six children. I believe he wrote this after one of our arguments the night before.

Dear Maribel,

Be patient with me.
All good things take TIME . . .
A rose is just a sticker bush until it is fertilized and watered, then it becomes a Flower.
A good book is only enjoyed when not rushed and Time is allowed to read it.
A sweet wine, through aging, fully blooms and is at its best when TIME is allowed to ferment it to perfection . . .
Be patient with me.
I can feel it coming and I will surprise you.
You have given me joy and a purpose in my life.
I love you always.

– Bill

And Bill said this to me on May 10, 2010, at another of our anniversary dinners at Il Terrazzo Carmine in downtown Seattle.

He had a glass of Barolo red wine, and I had Prosecco, which I refer to as the nectar of hummingbirds.

As he sipped his wine, he said, "Aah, this is the wine of contentment . . . [Bitter wine? I thought] . . . and yours, that is the wine of sweetness." He is such a poet! A man of this world, yet not so completely. His soul "swims in" my ether. So sweet, so poetic, so insightful, a true romantic at heart.

If, out of time, I could pick one moment and keep it shining, always new—of all the days that I have lived, I'd pick the moment I met you.

Anonymous

Chapter 5

Our Family Beginnings

*O*ur dream of buying old houses, fixing them up, and selling them for profit was altered to fit reality. No longer just a couple, our priorities quickly shifted to providing for a family of three: Bill, me, and our oldest son.

We both come from large families. I have nine siblings, and he had six in his family, including his parents. But neither one of us was prepared to start a family so early.

But where there is no family planning, there's "Family Planting" as the Filipinos would say.

We loved our first child so much. He changed our lives drastically, but he was also the apple of our eye as most first-borns are.

He was born prematurely, and we were told we could either lose the mother (meaning me) or our baby due to a condition called preeclampsia. We were both spared, thanks to GOD and modern medicine!

This first child started babbling before he could even form the words. He was so expressive and so animated and so fun to watch—he knew exactly what he was saying, although we did not. He was active and always exploring. He found himself in many skirmishes with the floor!

He loved to hide behind my houseplants and chew on the dirt. I used towels to cover the base of the plants to keep him from "snacking" on the soil. This condition is called pica—a craving and chewing of substances that have no nutritional value, such as ice, clay, soil, or paper. It is believed to be related to some nutritional deficiencies, like iron deficiency, for instance. He outgrew this, fortunately, before he was two years old. He is now in his late 30s. His interest is in real estate, and he was a real estate agent. He owned his own home at age 20. He is currently working for his Dad.

Shortly after our oldest son was born, our second child, a daughter, was on the way. I was in the healthiest condition when I was pregnant with her. She was a healthy, beautiful daughter with a distinct blondish red tuft of hair on the right side of her head. I had no pregnancy issues with her, only that she broke my tailbone on her way out, so I couldn't drive for six months! She was totally opposite our oldest child. She was quiet, easy to entreat, very observant, very smart, and content. She hardly ever cried as a baby.

All children are impressionable and believe everything their parents tell them. After all, we parents are their first teachers. But total belief and acceptance changes as kids grow up and they begin to learn things for themselves.

One evening during family dinnertime we talked about Easter eggs and Easter bunnies. I made a comment that if they (the kids) were good, the Easter Bunny would come and lay eggs for them. This daughter gave me a questioning look and said quietly,

"Bunnies don't lay eggs, Mom." I looked at my husband and said, "They do, don't they, honey?" My husband quickly answered and said, "No, they don't, honey."

"Oh . . . ," I honestly didn't know that bunnies don't lay eggs. "Oh, I guess not." I believe it was from this point on that my daughter may have lost some of her childhood awe and confidence in me. To this day, I feel like she doesn't believe everything I say.

I shared this true story with my nurse co-workers, and they all laughed and were amused that I truly didn't know that bunnies don't lay eggs! Didn't you learn that in your science classes? I said no. We didn't have bunnies in the Philippines, especially not Easter bunnies. We studied and dissected frogs and earthworms!

Not willing to settle and wanting to justify this rather stupid assumption on my part, I challenged my co-workers to ask two of our Filipino nurse co-workers. Huh! They, too, weren't sure if bunnies do or don't lay eggs! "There you go! I rest my case," I said feeling triumphant that I wasn't alone in this misconception. Actually, in my opinion, it was all due to cultural differences rather than scientific ignorance!

Easter in the Philippines is celebrated as a deeply spiritual holiday, not as a fun Easter egg hunt holiday for kids! There is quite a difference in focus and meaning. In the Philippines, Easter is only about the Resurrection of Jesus Christ. In fact, I remember being the special angel who was suspended in mid-air inside a giant flower with crepe paper as petals. The giant flower was supported by some scaffolding. On Easter Day, once I was in place inside the flower, a parade would pass by below me. When the Blessed Virgin Mary statue arrived under me, technicians then pulled a rope to open the flower and lower me (the angel) as if I were flying in mid-air and I would pick off the Blessed Virgin's veil covering her head and face and then sing Hallelujah and some triumphant song. I had to memorize the words but now I cannot recall what that song was!

Removing the veil from the statue of the Blessed Virgin signified that she was no longer mourning the death of her Son, Jesus Christ, as he was now resurrected.

That was Easter in the Philippines—absolutely no bunnies or eggs were involved!

I learned about some of this country's holiday traditions like Easter bunnies and egg hunting from my husband. Other little traditions that I carried on with our kids were leaving a plate of cookies and milk by the fireplace for Santa to eat when he comes down the chimney to leave gifts for the kids. And we also left bits of carrots and celery at the front doorstep for Santa's reindeer to snack on. Of course, I knew this was just for fun!

The children, however, believed that they did hear Santa's sleigh bells in the middle of the night as he stopped by our house. When my oldest daughter was a little older, she carried on this little Christmas tradition of milk and cookies for Santa and carrots and celery at the front door for Santa's reindeer. She did not tell the younger kids that it was all just pretending. Again, I didn't learn about any of this growing up in the Philippines because, of course, being in the tropics, we don't have chimneys or fireplaces. I learned about all this here in the United States.

I'm sharing this information as I look back at this stage of my life. These little traditions were fun for our children, and I think it's good to have some degree of "fairy tale" to spice up children's lives and imagination.

My oldest daughter is my left-brained child. She is smart, logical, methodical, and resourceful, and she was very responsible at an early age. She now has a master's degree in psychology and is a counselor. She is married with three beautiful daughters.

A year and a half after our second child was born, our third child arrived. He came with a perfect, round bald head, but he was too big and positioned the wrong way. So, after more than 12 hours of labor and being placed on a 100% oxygen face mask, the doctors decided to do another C-section. This third baby's presentation was occiput posterior (head down, but facing front instead of toward my back), so his big head had a difficult time passing through the birth canal and my labor was too long and presenting a medical problem for the baby. My first child was also a C-section because he was Frank breech presentation meaning he was in danger of coming out butt-first with his legs near his ears. This third child is now married with three children. He also works for his Dad.

I decided to go to work when our third child was one and a half years old. It wasn't until three years and three months later that our fourth child was born. Again, I was perfectly healthy throughout this beautiful pregnancy, but my baby's head was positioned wrongly, and our high-risk specialist obstetrician felt confident in performing his special maneuver of turning the baby's head. My husband and sister-in-law who were present nearly fainted as they had never seen such a gory delivery! My son was a successful forceps delivery—a strong handsome robust baby with bruises all over his head and temples. He graduated high school and went on to university. After serving a two-year mission in our church, he went back to school and took a degree in business management. He is a world traveler and in 2021–2022 toured four countries in Europe (Spain, Italy, France, and Greece).

Our fifth child came next. We knew she was a girl by amniocentesis. I was 35 years old by then and this was the protocol. She was a scheduled C-section, now the third of such a type of delivery that I had had.

With this C-section, I experienced such excruciating pain in my incision. This had never happened before. I thought I had done it all, but apparently not. Morphine injections dulled the pain for a bit, but then it would come back with a vengeance.

Finally, I was given intravenous fentanyl. It was the only medication that took the pain away effectively and put me to sleep. I was able to rest through the night and still be fairly pain-free as I woke up the following morning, only to find myself itching all over! I remember the doctor asking me how I was feeling that morning, one day post-delivery, and I said happily, "I'm good!" while I was scratching my body, face, and all over my head!

The doctor looked at me with an amused expression on his face. Later on, I realized why. I must have looked to him like a dog with fleas! I laughed as I didn't care as long as I was pain-free, and the baby was born healthy with a full head of hair that was unusually long for a newborn!

This child, a girl, was in second grade when we moved to Briarwood in East Renton Highlands, the area where we still live. She now has a Bachelor of Science degree in Nursing and is married with five children. The most recent child was born a couple of years ago.

Ten months later, I delivered, by emergency, our sixth child. He was nearly born on the bus on my way home from work! Because he wasn't due for a couple more months, I was in total surprise when I started my labor without showing signs other than extreme pain in my abdomen.

It was the year when Seattle had a severe winter snowstorm that covered the streets for weeks. Thick-packed snow that turned icy made driving dangerous, thus, I took the bus to and from work at Harborview. The Metro buses only went to Chinatown, so after getting off my bus, I had to walk those hills that are between Chinatown and Harborview. I had quite the daily workout.

I had one prenatal check with this last baby before he was born as I wasn't aware I was pregnant. I thought my body just hadn't returned to normal after my previous, fifth child was born.

"Fertile Myrtle" was at it again! I was exhausted and half-embarrassed for not heeding my doctor's advice to allow my body to heal. He had counseled me to not have babies for a while.

My husband drove me to the hospital in his car with no snow tires or chains! As he stopped at every light, I screamed in extreme pain and clawed at him as he was driving. A mad woman is on board! I'm sure that's what people would have thought if they could have seen into the car and heard my screams. Fortunately, this was in the middle of winter, and it was quite dark in the early evening.

When we arrived at the hospital, I was wheeled quickly to my room. Our doctor had prepared us mentally for what to expect. An intensive care team was waiting and appraised my situation—that I was two months early and that I was already 5.5 centimeters dilated. The plan was to give me medication to stop the contractions and put me on bedrest until the baby was closer to his due date. But contractions and dilation were progressing quickly, so I was prepped to have the baby that night.

As the anesthesiologist gave his instructions for me to go on my side and curl up like a cat, I had one very strong contraction. I couldn't help but push. And in one big grunt, my baby was born with poor Apgar scores. Fortunately, the intensive care team was there, and the baby was quickly attended to and placed in a tent. He was too weak to suck so he had to be given or fed formula via an oral gastric feeding tube connected to his stomach.

★ ★ ★

This was a time of awakening and much hardship on our family—mentally, emotionally, and physically. We had our church elders give a blessing of health and healing for our baby boy who was born prematurely with all the risks a premature baby was subject to. Every day he lived was gold to us. We couldn't take him home with us for obvious reasons, but every day without fail, I came to feed him breast milk via his oral gastric tube early in the morning after dropping off the other kids to school and leaving the other three with our in-home babysitter. Then, I would go back home to attend to our five older kids in the afternoon and eventually load them all up in the car with Bill so we could go see their little baby brother in the evening until visiting hours were over. We wanted to be there and stay with him as long as we could and as long as was allowed according to the hospital visiting hours.

Our eldest daughter remembers feeling so sad and disappointed when I came home without our baby. She cried and quietly went to her room. Every day was a struggle and a joy at the same time that our baby boy was getting better. At one point the doctors told us that it wasn't uncommon for babies born this early to have necrotic bowel syndrome or necrotizing enterocolitis. This is a condition caused by an internal infection that the baby can't fight. We were surprised when we found out that the baby next to ours in the nursery had died the same day we were told of the possibility of this risk.

After two months in the hospital, our baby's appetite and strength were improving a lot with the colostrum-rich breast milk I was feeding him daily and as often as needed. He was picking up weight, a good sign that he was ready to be discharged home soon.

These two months seemed to us like forever—we couldn't wait to bring him home! The day we did was a day of gratitude and great joy for our whole family of six kids. Now, finally, we felt complete. ☺

Our youngest went on to college and got his Associates of Arts degree. Then, he served a two-year mission with our church. Currently, he works for his Dad in the office.

Due to childbirth challenges and difficulties on my part, Bill and I decided that six kids were enough to keep us busy, so he got "fixed"—an easier procedure for him than for me.

Chapter 6

Home Life With Six

"where the rubber meets the road"

*A*s a foreigner with English as my second language, I've found that even after so many years of speaking the language, idioms used commonly by first-hand English speakers often don't make sense to me.

I used to say to my co-workers: "Knowledge is flat, as in, it has no real depth. But WISDOM comes through experience."

As such, the particular idiom "where the rubber meets the road" has only distilled through and crystallized in my understanding (as a nonnative English speaker) by living and experiencing what it has felt like to press on and ride through the bumpy roads that come with raising our family of six children.

I figured if my Mom could handle raising ten children, I, too, could do it, and with fewer kids! I did not consider that raising a family in the United States and raising a family in the Philippines would be so different—in more ways than one. The two places are literally continents apart. In the Philippines, you have a lot of physical help and support, and, by U.S. standards, having child-care and maids is quite inexpensive. In the U.S., the extended family is often unavailable because everyone is working and busy with their own lives. Plus, in the U.S., childcare costs an arm and a leg. I think we all know that. So, I had to learn the hard way!

Bill and I quickly added six kids to our family within a ten-year period between the early 80s and the early 90s. No one was counting or planning. We were just busy living life as it came. Although we had many fun memorable moments with each child and life was always so hectic, the years did not pass by fast enough. My husband and I were outnumbered. It was a relief when all the kids were grown up.

Our priorities were obviously altered from our original dream of personal pursuits and accomplishments to that of focusing solely on our fast-growing family. We needed a bigger home, so we moved from Bill's first fixer-upper to a home with four bedrooms. This was possible because Bill put the word out to his friends and co-workers. Foregoing the help of realtors or the stress of looking for a house, Bill reached out to a guy who he knew years ago while working for Benjamin's restaurant in Bellevue. This friend of his owned a successful Chinese restaurant—Mayflower of China in Southcenter—and he partnered with his brother in building houses. This old friend happened to be looking to sell his home. Bill was very excited and couldn't wait for me to see the house. On his lunch hour, his friend showed it to us. I fell in love at first sight. I brought my Mom to see it and she readily approved! The next day, we signed papers and put our money down.

However, there was one glitch to this golden opportunity. Before we could move in, we had to wait six months while the owner was building his new home.

At the time, I was pregnant with my third child, but I loved the house so much, I was willing to wait. But then, six months passed, and we were still waiting. My patience grew thin as I was approaching the third trimester of this third baby. After waiting seven months, we finally moved in. Our new home was all furnished and ready only one month prior to the birth of our third child. It was worth the wait!

About that home of ours in Beacon Hill—it had so many lovely amenities, which we didn't have with our first house. It was multilevel with a sunken living room with a high ceiling and a solarium off the kitchen with ceiling to floor windows. This was a place to relax after dinner and where we could see planes through the glass roof. We could also watch the kids play basketball in the backyard from a high vantage point. It was really beautiful and quite charming. We later added an eight-person hot tub right underneath the master bedroom deck, something Bill really loved, especially on snow days. We have fun memories of living in that house while our children grew up.

We lived in the home in Beacon Hill until our sixth child finished kindergarten and our oldest graduated from sixth grade. From the time we moved into that Beacon Hill neighborhood, there was never a dull moment. There were lots of kids around from multi-ethnic families—Black, white, Chinese, Filipino, Japanese, and mixed-race. Our children fit right in.

This was never a consideration, but it just so happened that way: the kids in the immediate homes soon found our place to be the "neighborhood hang-out." Every day without fail, we would have at least four to five kids playing with ours.

I didn't mind because I was a stay-at-home mom at the time and my kids enjoyed having lots of playmates. In the summer, the kids would ride their low bikes on our driveway or play in the little clubhouse Bill built for them. As they got a little older, they would play hoops in the back yard. We went through a menagerie of pets as if the number of kids were not enough. We had puppies, mini-turtles, chickens, which, of course, were cute when they were chicks and no longer cute when the kids had to learn to clean their coop! Or when the turtles crawled into the heating vent and refused to be rescued! It was quite an ordeal using a coat hanger to try to get them out until I found a wiser way to prod them out of their hiding place on their own accord by turning the furnaces up on high. Only then did the turtles decide to crawl up and out of the vent before getting cooked!

We had two bunnies that I had gotten from one of my co-workers. I had wondered why they didn't multiply as I was told bunnies do very quickly. I didn't realize then they couldn't because they were the same sex! Well, how was I supposed to know? I didn't inspect them! I had just assumed they would get together and multiply. Oh, these little nuisances!

We had two goats, cute little ones Bill brought home one day from Maple Valley. They were meant to naturally clean the bramble of bushes immediately outside our fenced-in backyard, which was part of our property. One afternoon, our oldest son was walking home from school with his classmate. His classmate said laughing, "Oh look, you have a goat in your backyard!" Embarrassed, our son said, "No, it's a dog!" Then the goat started shooting out small pellets from its behind and they both cracked up laughing at the goat as it stood proudly on top of a huge rock among the bushes. My husband took the goats back to their owners once they successfully did their mission of clearing out the brambles beyond our fence.

We also had a special cockatiel we called "Goldie." She literally knocked on our glass sliding door with her beak to be let into our house. That's how we came to adopt her. We didn't buy a cage because she was very smart and tame. Whenever she needed a drink of water, she would go to our kitchen sink and alight on our arm and drink from the faucet as we were holding her. I let her fly freely in the house. The kids loved it until we realized she was making too much mess to clean up after. We had her for probably a couple of years until she escaped out of our home one summer, never to be seen again.

Apparently, as the kids got a little older, they would sneak out into the bramble of blackberry bushes right outside our fenced-in basketball court where they made a little hole to crawl through and played on a plank of dry plywood. There they found all sorts of little creatures I didn't want inside our home. One day my little three-year-old came into the house and showed me what he found: two potato bugs rolled up like little black balls. I smiled and then screamed in surprise as he put his hand in his pocket and said, "I got some muy, Mamma!" I nearly had a heart attack as he released six more of those little black potato bugs and they started crawling. I had never come across those before in my life, so they took me by surprise!

"It's okay, Mamma, they won't bite you," my three-year-old assured me as he crouched down to pick them all up off my white carpet! "Yikes!" I thought. What treasures do these little ones find. They are like cats that leave unwanted gifts at your front door!

More surprises . . . kids say the funniest things . . .

I had all of my first three kids in bottles and diapers at one point. I didn't believe in setting deadlines for weaning them until they were ready. My Mom didn't do that either and we all turned out just fine. I remember when we were able to eat "table food"—that's when we were weaned naturally. To make it easy for me, I would line up their bottles on the three side shelves of the refrigerator. The highest shelf for the oldest, the middle shelf for our second child, and the lowest shelf for our little toddler. One night our toddler came running into our room huffing in fright, "Mamma, there's a munter (monster) in the fridge!" I thought he must have been having a nightmare!

I went to the fridge to fetch his bottle for him and sure enough, as I opened the fridge, little eyes moved with their antennas—I had forgotten that Bill had come home with three live lobsters. He put them in an open pot on the bottom shelf of the fridge!

Their huge pinchers were bound together in rubber bands to keep them from crawling out and pinching. My little toddler was not imagining things. At his eye level, these creatures must have looked like dangerous, scary monsters, especially when their beady eyes and antennas moved!

All our kids attended St. George Parish School until our oldest child graduated from there and our youngest, the sixth child, was in kindergarten. It was customary for that school to ask the pupils if they had any special requests to pray for someone sick or in need. Our youngest one promptly raised his hand and told his teacher, "My Mom is dying." So, he got his whole class to pray for me. When I went to pick up the kids from school, his teacher made a point to come out, kindly approach, and inform me that her class prayed for me that day.

Thinking nothing of it, I thanked her and said, "That's so sweet of you." The teacher went on to probe politely in order to find out what I might be dying of so they could be more specific with their prayer requests.

"Are you okay?" she asked me. I told her I was just so tired and exhausted. Finally, the teacher told me what Shawn, our little kindergartener, had said. "Oh, my gosh!" I exclaimed. I burst out laughing when I realized that Shawn had overheard me say, "Lord, have mercy! I'm dying!" He took that to mean literally.

"My poor kid," I told the teacher. "I'm so sorry. That's just my expression for when I feel overwhelmed! I'm not sick with anything!" Relieved, the teacher had a good laugh along with me. Our kids say the darnedest things.

Another time, I overheard our kids having a conversation with our new neighbor's daughter who was close in age to our kids. Her mom was an elementary school principal and she herself was pretty smart for her age. She told my kids she was a Blackfoot Indian. Curious, one of my kids said, "Let's see!" The girl must have shown them her feet, and my kids all chimed in and said, "You're not a Blackfoot Indian! Your feet are white!"

Raising a multi-cultural family can sometimes pose some confusing communication. I was already an adult when I came to this country and although I learned to speak the language well, I was still unfamiliar with a lot of expressions. One day our fourth child came to me after he visited our neighbor and asked for a cup of sugar. I readily obliged and gave him a cup of sugar to take back to our neighbor. Shortly after, the doorbell rang and here was my neighbor bringing back the cup of sugar that my son had just brought to her. She was laughing. She was so amused at my kid for bringing a cup of sugar to her house.

I said, "Oh, Charlie said you needed a cup of sugar!" Our neighbor explained what she meant. She was referring to how cute and adorable our little Charlie was! So, she said to him, "Give me a cup of that sugar!" This neighbor was from down South. Little did she know that I was not familiar with that expression either. Like mother, like son!

* ★ *

Funny no more . . .

Raising a family of six kids can be quite fun but challenging in many ways. With growing kids of all ages come growing pains due to their endless energy, curiosity, and avid-thirst for exploration.

Our oldest child was the most curious explorer. One afternoon, suddenly I heard this blood curdling scream coming from the solarium. I ran from my room to find that our oldest child had burned his mouth—his lower lip was an explosion of white flesh and there was blood trickling down his chin. I was beside myself! I found out that he had bitten the extension cord from the floor lamp while it was still plugged into the electrical outlet.

It was hard for me to leave our Beacon Hill house because we had so many memorable moments there. But we needed to as the kids got older, and we had to relocate for better schooling. After months of house hunting and much frustration, we finally found this home in Briarwood, a little community between Renton and Issaquah. It's such a perfect spot, and we still live here. In Briarwood, all our kids could go to school in the excellent Issaquah school district—only a few miles from our home. We moved here in the late 90s, only one month prior to Mama Aning's passing away. She never got to see this house.

Here's a summary of our struggles in having a family with six kids, with hopefully some inspiration for how to love and endure.

The road was always bumpy because: (1) it was hard to find reliable caretakers for our kids who satisfied our expectations, (2) we had financial hardships and needed to prioritize expenditures to make ends meet, (3) we were always suffering from a lack of physical, mental, and emotional energy and stamina, (4) it was hard to find quality time for each child, and this led to (5) strained relationships, especially between Bill and me.

Due to the lack of time for each other, we were often too tired to have fun. It was hard to find a balance, and we so needed that. This led to our inability to see the big picture at times and adjust our needs and expectations. We tended to feel unequally yoked. I felt overworked and overwhelmed without the help of Bill at home. In other words, home life was a constant testing ground, where the rubber met the road and the going was so rough and, at times, all four tires were flat!

Eventually, Bill and I realized we were bound together by something stronger than our own personal needs and complaints. We discovered our love was of a deeper kind—our commitment.

So, we became determined to follow this wise advice:

Never let a problem to be solved become more important than a person to be loved.

President Thomas S. Monson in
"Finding Joy in the Journey" from a Conference Report,
October 2008

I so love this statement as a reminder that no matter how difficult it is at times to show love instead of annoyance, the person to be loved is indeed far more important than a circumstance to be solved.

The things we did to honor our commitment to each other and to resolve our issues were:

1. We adjusted our expectations.

2. We accepted our needs and prioritized them.

3. We accepted our circumstances—what was what and made do with what we had.

4. We sought Grace through prayer and perseverance.

5. We strengthened our spiritual muscles.

6. We strengthened our faith through prayer.

7. We endured and reminded ourselves of our commitment daily.

Chapter 7

My Work: Nursing

Part 1
A Calling

The human spirit is transformed
when we choose
a vocation that serves others—
like NURSING.

MBC

$\mathcal{I}$ believe Nursing is one of the most benevolent and revered professions there is in life.

Nursing was ingrained in me ever since I can remember. Having grown up and having been raised in a medical family, this was a way of life. I remember as a first grader my role in a little skit presented to the whole town at the end of the school year was as a NURSE. My parents were tickled pink and after that little performance everyone in town would tease me and say with a big smile: "Nurse, Nurse, I need help!"

My Dad had a clinic on the first floor of our home. I remember treating my friends' wounds or scratches with Merthiolate or Mercurochrome, which was standard for those types of minor skin injuries. Then, I would cover the injury with 2x2 gauze and secure it with special medical tape. We had no band aids at that time.

I was fascinated by how the wounds I treated would heal the next day as if nothing had ever been there . . . magic! My friends trusted me, and I enjoyed taking care of them.

Every Sunday was a big clinic day for my Dad, which also corresponded to Mercado Day, or Big Market Day. Actually, all four towns that comprise Camotes Island participated in Mercado

Day. It was a special day to sell goods to people and to shop and be seen by others.

Not everyone could afford to pay monetarily. People in need of care from the mountains and neighboring towns would bring chickens, fruits, root vegetables, other veggies, corn, Filipino-style homemade baked goods, rice, budbud, fried bananas and plantains, or sacks of raw peanuts as a way to thank my Dad and pay for their treatment. In turn, sometimes we would feed these people with our kind of food—rice, bas-oy (beef soup), calderetta (goat meat), and bifsteck (thinly-sliced fried beef). They loved my Dad. They loved our family.

So, my chosen profession—Nursing—this type of humanitarian practice and work—was ingrained in me: feed the poor among us, heal the sick who come, whoever they may be. And behind the medical and nursing practice was always the HEART with which people were being treated.

This early childhood experience helped shape my future career as a Nurse. It became my chosen profession once I was old enough to make a serious decision on which career path to follow after high school. I took my precollege test while attending Queen Anne High School, which was administered at Seattle University's Peugeot Hall. I remember feeling scared and intimidated by my own anxiety over English as my second language as well as being new in this country and totally overwhelmed by the size of the University's campus. All that aside, I scored highest toward the humanities career path. That put me straight in line with nursing. I applied to the University of Washington School of Nursing Program. I was accepted and enrolled in pre-nursing classes.

I had a mixture of excitement, anxiety, and more excitement as I embarked on a clear path to young adulthood.

Part 2

A Sudden Detour — The Church

*T*here was a detour on this Nursing journey.

Close to graduation, I met a group that was part of a religious organization called the Unification Church. A lay-missionary from
France who was proselytizing at the University of Washington
campus approached me and, out of the blue, interrupted my
thoughts and blurted out a rhetorical question, which blew me
away! "Do you believe in GOD?"

She waited for my response. Then, in her thick French accent,
proceeded to ask, "Do you think a loving GOD would allow all
this sadness in the world to happen because of disunity among its
people? Wouldn't it be ideal if we could somehow change that?"
Next, I got hooked because she invited me to go to a class, which
would give me the answers. Nestled among sorority buildings
and apartments in the UW campus vicinity was the Unification
Church facility. I was greeted with smiles, given a simple sandwich and water for lunch, then invited to listen to a talk about
their doctrinal beliefs referred to as the Divine Principle.

They didn't give me the lessons all at once—just a chapter at a
time with some scientific facts, which made sense to me. I attended the lessons on and off depending on my class schedule.
Anne Marie, which was this French "sister's" name, was persistent

with her follow-up proselytizing. Eventually, I became a regular attendee at these lessons and dinner programs, which involved singing and meeting all kinds of people of different nationalities and from different parts of the world.

These people were very nice; some were I presumed students attending the University of Washington. Anne Marie herself was studying in the pre-med program. My focus in life soon was split between becoming a professional nurse by finishing school or being part of a higher calling to bring peace and unity to this world through a unifying principle espoused by the Unification Church.

Eventually, much to my family's disapproval, I attended a weekend workshop these people sponsored in which the entire Divine Principle was taught. I had a lot of questions, which sprung out of new knowledge that threatened my preconceived Christian beliefs based on my Catholic upbringing. My paradigm was being challenged and "threatened," so to speak. But a voice inside me reminded me of this scripture: "Ye shall know them by their fruits." And I had no reason to disbelieve these people because they seemed to be genuinely sincere, and they lived clean, physical, and spiritual lives according to their principles and beliefs. It wasn't long before I found an affinity with them. This spiritual journey derailed my nursing career path as I decided to put it at a higher priority over my schooling.

Amidst a lot of my youthful inexperience and ambivalence over which path was best to follow, that of my personal pursuit to finish Nursing or the selfless act of being a missionary, I chose the higher calling, that of a missionary. I was then sent as one of the candidates or new recruits to the seminary in Upstate New York in Barrytown for further training.

Barrytown is an idyllic little hamlet in the town of Red Hook, Dutchess Country, New York. It's a totally peaceful, beautiful place with rolling hills, pine trees, and rich green foliage growing on the banks of the great Hudson River. The setting totally imbued a spiritual awakening of the senses—one that I could truly attribute to the peace that only Mother Nature could inspire—a perfect setting for a rich spiritual awakening.

Everyone was assigned to teams with a Team Leader—and there was strict separation of living quarters by gender. Furthermore, there was a strict adherence to a modest dress code including shoulder length hair for girls and no facial hair and well-trimmed short hair for men.

Each member was kept busy doing the tasks assigned to whichever team they belonged to. We learned a lot from those different divisions or assignments—cooking, farming, cleaning, restoring old buildings, fundraising, and door-to-door missionary work or proselytizing. It was hard work but also a lot of fun because we got to meet and work with all kinds of people from all over the world. Language was not an issue because only a few Korean artists or performers did not speak English. The Rev. Sun Myung Moon, the Korean founder of the Unification Church, did not speak English either. But his teachings were taught and written in English. He lived near enough to Barrytown to visit on special occasions and I saw him several times. However, he did not commune with the members on a daily basis. Whenever he spoke to the whole congregation of followers, he always had a very well-educated interpreter beside him. Rev. Moon was revered by many if not all, and we understood the principles he taught were sound and marvelous. We were all part of a global happening that started small in South Korea and was now blossoming globally to change the world and unify all mankind, thus, the church was called The Unification Church. And each Team was a Family.

The training was very well organized with a strict schedule to follow.

We all woke up bright and early at 5:30 am every morning for personal prayer in the chapel. My first impression was one of great reverence to a GOD we prayed to in silence within our own thoughts and hearts. After a while, meaning months, I was curious if anyone was as sleepy as I was with my forehead on the floor and my knees and legs firmly planted on the cold floors of the chapel. Once, I was rudely awakened by some loud snoring among the "prayerful" attendees/brothers and sisters. Shocked, and to my surprise, several were asleep with their foreheads on the floor and sitting on their thighs and bums. Wow, that's terrible, I thought. Then I realized I couldn't judge because I too was about to fall asleep!

After this early morning ritual, we would go back to our group quarters—sisters with sisters and the brothers in a different building. We then would change into exercise clothes for the 30-minute outdoor morning exercise and breathe the fresh air in this lush green setting of Barrytown, New York, beside the Hudson River.

Then we would prepare for the day—there was a huge community shower room shared by all sisters. This was new for me (!) as I was brought up to be private in these matters. I looked around and no one seemed to be curious about other people showering beside them. I was the only one with such a "cultural shock" from my normal practice. I got used to it after a while.

Then, after everyone was dressed, we would all go together again in teams, separate tables for each team, to enjoy a huge breakfast prepared by the Kitchen Team. All food or most may have been grown right there at that huge Barrytown estate with acres and acres of farmland and rolling hills. I didn't see any livestock other than chickens.

After breakfast, there was the teaching of what was called the Divine Principle. Everyone assembled in the big auditorium to listen and learn from special speakers who taught words of wisdom for everyday living and spiritual life.

One particular "regular" teacher that stood out for me was a diminutive man named Mr. Sato. He spoke very softly, sometimes in hushed tones. Due to his Japanese accent, one had to really strain to hear him. But his words carried a lot of weight. He spoke words of wisdom that without a doubt penetrated the hearts and minds of those who listened. The whole auditorium would be so hushed and NO ONE, as I looked around in my curiosity, was asleep like they were at the chapel. Mr. Sato shared with us the meat and bones of why we were there—why we wanted to be part of that church and how we came to be members.

I was in training for six months.

Mr. Sato, the great diminutive teacher, taught with a great heart and a Big Mind. He was close to Rev. Sun Myung Moon and was highly respected in the church. I joined in 1976 when the church was burgeoning in size as well as popularity and unpopularity. There was a lot of negative press that the members were being subjected to mental-physical and emotional torture (i.e., indoctrination, as they called it) and were kept against their will. The "they" were "enemies" of the church who were against this new church movement.

To be truly honest, nothing of the sort could be farther from the truth.

True, we were taught new things and new perspectives but based on mainstream Christian beliefs. Catholics and Protestants were no longer able to inspire GOD's truth and doing good based on faith and true believing. The Old Christian churches were losing their grip on a great number of young people due to their ritualistic teachings, which had lost meaning in their present world.

"You can't put new wine in old skins, or the container will burst." And, yes, a lot of churches and families were in uproar against the new teachings of this new church, including my very own family.

After our six-month training in Barrytown, we new trainees were sent to our assigned states and cities throughout the U.S. I was assigned to Las Vegas and Lake Tahoe in Nevada to be a full-time missionary.

I brought in two members from there. Then in 1976, the church had its biggest rally at the Washington, D.C. monument.

After the big Washington Monument rally, we all went to the NY-Manhattan area where the Unification Church had a huge building—I can't recall what it was called, but I believe this is where the newly-established Unification Church center and newspaper circulars offices were located. We stayed here until new assignments were prefigured for all of us. I was reassigned to go back to Washington, D.C., where once again we lived in "family units" headed by a Papasan and a Mamasan. I also ended up traveling to nearby states like Maryland, Virginia, Massachusetts, and I enjoyed a one-week stay in Vermont. In Massachusetts, I met a girl from MIT who eventually joined the church and got "matched" or married and went on to have a family.

Our meeting house in Washington, D.C., was located on Church Street, and, with the leadership of the Papasan and Mamasan duo, the needs of each member were met. The Papasan and Mamasan were a "blessed couple" or matched in a mass wedding by the Rev. Sun Myung Moon.

Food, shelter, clothing, and medical needs were all taken care of by the church. We were continuously taught the Divine

Principle, and, in turn, we proselytized to the public to bring in more members by invitation.

Approaching my third year in the church in 1978 (1976, 1977, and 1978), I had a strong longing to come back home to Seattle and finish my nursing education. The Mamasan and Papasan of my Family Unit in Washington, D.C., tried to convince me to stay and offered to pay for my nursing education. They also tried to suggest that I was eligible to be "matched," meaning matched in marriage. I declined. At this point, with nearly three years devoted to the Church, my mind was made up to go back home to my family.

By 1978, I was accepted to and re-enrolled in the UW School of Nursing Program.

I eventually graduated from the nursing program, married Bill, and we started a family right away. Bill and I both decided that I should stay home to raise our family. So, I never practiced or went to work as a nurse until the kids were older, and I was inspired to do so by my Mom.

Part 3

Work—A Necessity and a Blessing

$\mathcal{I}$t was late in the afternoon when my Mom stopped by for a surprise visit to our home in Beacon Hill. I was physically exhausted and emotionally frayed. My home was always kept in order even with three little kids. I had my daily routine. Making sure their needs were met as well as having a nice, clean, orderly home, as I had been taught to have by example from my Mother, were top priorities for me.

But—those busy explorative years of children—having a clean home was like, to borrow someone else's expression, brushing your teeth and eating chocolate chip cookies at the same time! OMG! I could totally relate to that!

The joy of being a mother was overshadowed by my obsession with keeping my home nice, clean, and orderly. Of course, the children had no clue, but when my Mother walked in that afternoon to visit me, she knew immediately how I was doing. Juggling little kids and a home with the self-imposed expectation to keep it tidy at all times had taken its toll on my physical appearance. I was still in my pj's! My Mom did remark how beautifully I had kept our home, and she noted that the children were well-dressed and happy.

When we sat down and had some tea and cookies, she offered her motherly words of wisdom given her observation of me neglecting my own personal appearance—pj's still into the late afternoon? Hmmm. She said I should really consider working part-time, at least to keep up with my nursing degree, which I had worked hard to attain. Also, she suggested that there might be a time limit as to how long post-graduation my BSN-RN (Bachelor of Science in Nursing-Registered Nurse) degree would be valid.

"You would not want to be going back to take a refresher course would you?" she asked.

After my Mom left, this thought rolled through my mind several times. No. Definitely not! I wouldn't want to waste those years of education without putting them to use. So, I put this question up for discussion with Bill over dinner that night. He was not at all welcoming of the idea of me pursuing my career outside the home instead of being a housewife and a mother! He felt very strongly that my place was at home nurturing our children versus working at a career. To quote him, if my memory serves me right, he said, "Had I known you were going to be a career woman, I wouldn't have married you."

Although his parents were divorced, he grew up in a traditional family where the husband went to work to provide, and the mother stayed home to take care of the family's needs and the children.

I too grew up like that until our family moved to this country and, out of necessity, my Mom had to go to work full-time. Of course, having relocated from the Philippines to the U.S. and having those many children of school age was quite a financial challenge and undertaking. Fortunately, my Mom had no problem getting full-time employment at the University of Washington Hospital as an anesthesia tech. This was because of her familiarity with the medical field and her medical background. And she had a strong personal reference from my aunt, who was already working there.

At this point in our life, Bill and I were doing fine financially, and the kids were still too young to be left at home. We had no back-up plan for childcare.

So, pursuing a nursing career outside of the home was put on hold. Still, the idea of practicing nursing had piqued my interest, and I kept talking about it to Bill. The time did finally come when Bill opened up to the idea and said if I could find someone as a "live-in nanny" to keep the kids in our home rather than a daycare or someone else's home, pursuing nursing would be fine.

In the meantime, I sent my applications to different hospital facilities in the area. I had a few interviews but never progressed to a second interview. The letters I received back from those hospitals said "overqualified" or "under qualified." You see, as a nursing student, I never worked because my parents said to focus on my studies, and they paid for all my nursing education at the University of Washington. This didn't hurt me, but in the long run, I realized it did hurt me in that part of the "points" to score employability was "experience"—of which I had none! My co-grads had immediate employment after school because they had put their foot in by working at a nursing home or part-time at a hospital while they were pursuing their education. So, this served as "experience" for them. And the people they worked with knew them and gave them immediate references. As for me, I was an unknown entity and, therefore, considered to be as experienced as a fresh new graduate. And given the time between my graduation to when I was seeking employment also worked against me for being seen as viable for immediate employment. Harborview Medical Center (HMC), then called Harborview Hospital, was never one of the places I dreamed of working. I applied to Virginia Mason, Swedish Hospital, Providence Hospital, and the V.A. Hospital. I don't think the Valley Medical Center was around then. There was also the Military Hospital and, last but not least, the Western State Hospital in Steilacoom, Tacoma, a mental hospital for severely sick patients with psychiatric disorders.

Another thing I learned in filling out applications is that the availability of a prospective employee is important—e.g., date available to work, shift preferences, and salary. I would write in DAY SHIFT only, Mon→Fri, and no weekends. Available times: I don't remember what I wrote in here!

My concern became more apparent after several months of waiting for a positive response from these facilities I applied to. I shared this concern with my husband whose work experience far exceeded mine! He worked out of necessity at age 13 years when, as a product of divorced parents, he had to provide for himself and his brother. Nothing was below him—he was not afraid to work. He had to! He experienced homelessness; he experienced being hungry. He experienced what it was like having a family but feeling unwelcome on both sides because of a bitter divorce. He could count on no one but himself and his older brother, Harry.

My husband had wise suggestions on how to fill out my employment application to enhance my chances of being a promising prospective employee. I took his counsel and, sure enough, I got an encouraging letter from HMC. I had written down that I was available for employment at any time and for any shift they wanted to put me in! I was ready, willing, and able to start anytime!

My references were all from my academic years. My first reference was my last instructor in Public Health Nursing who happened to be the Quality Assurance Director of Nursing at Harborview at the time I sent my application. My second reference was another nursing instructor known for her role in the development of the hyperbaric chamber at Virginia Mason. My last reference was my psychology instructor who later became the Nursing Union President. I was very fortunate to have had great relationships with these instructors who put in a good word for me as far as my credibility and ability to pick up where I left off was concerned. I know this was no coincidence but rather an answer to my prayers for getting hired so I did not have to waste my nursing degree or be made to take refresher courses. This job was a necessity.

I was hired in November 1986.

Nursing is not merely a skill set or a body of knowledge to study and train for. It is a gift to the one who becomes a Nurse as well as a gift to those he/she has the privilege of serving and working with. Nursing, I must say, is truly a GIFT from GOD!

If we are focused and aware, we become GOD's hands at work. In this sense, Nursing is truly a blessing.

I feel fortunate to have chosen this profession because how often can one honestly say they love their work and get paid for it? Nursing is very fulfilling—a mission more than just a job.

One of the very first tenets I learned in Basic Nursing Fundamentals was the word "RAPPORT." It's a word with French origins and it means to have a good understanding of someone or the ability to communicate well with them. We were taught that establishing a good rapport with our patients builds trust and a great foundation for a healing relationship. I believe being compassionate is something that we are born with—or, for some, compassion can be developed in order to have empathy toward those you take care of. Empathy connects us with our patients on a deeper level, which the patients can feel, and they love you for it, because they trust that you are truly there for them and will advocate for them to the medical team.

The patients feel "safe" when a Nurse is able to explain to them what the doctor means with a certain diagnosis, different treatments, and a prognosis in layman terms that are easy to understand and relatable. The patients then feel they are being treated as precious, invaluable human beings, not just a number or a diagnosis or a "DIS-EASE."

When this nurse-patient connection happens, the patient becomes emotionally engaged with their Treatment Team, which includes all the involved doctors and nurses, and they become empowered to get well. Of course, there are multifactorial circumstances that affect the eventual outcome of the hospitalization experience. However, in the process of the patient's journey while he or she is under your nursing care, TIME is well spent because you are making someone more comfortable and happier, and not alone in their infirmities. And for the nurse caregiver, the nurse-patient connection gives substance and meaning and purpose to his or her work.

In the 30-year term that I worked as a Nurse at Harborview, the most meaningful and fulfilling years were the first 20 years. The advent of technology—the cellphones for nurses, the computers, and the adherence to checklists and "computer-measured tasks"—gave way to a "hands-off" versus HANDS-ON style of Nursing. The technology was meant initially to save time so caretakers could be more available to the patients. However, looking at my entire experience from the point of view of someone who is retired—a total of three decades in the practice—has shown me, in my own opinion, that technology has taken nurses and doctors AWAY from the patient's bedside. I think in more ways than one, the advent of technology dependence has given rise to the absence of RAPPORT and less warmth, personal attention, and caring.

I worked from November 1986 to December 2016—a 30-year-span, which I consider to be a badge of honor full of life experiences. Without Nursing, I would never have had the privilege of knowing, learning, and meeting many kinds of people from all strata of life. I'm grateful to those who mentored me—some have passed on to the next life. I give a special mention to the BEST NURSE and mentor ever! She was a "10," a brilliant spot in my life as a Nurse. And to another bright and "funny" nurse mentor as well—GOD bless you in your spiritual journey now in Heaven. I owe a lot to my very first preceptor, who later became my nurse manager and was for several years. She valued my contribution to our unit, including sending me to represent our unit 4 East, for HMC's Recruitment and Retention Group. Consequently, the Nurse Education Department asked me to participate in their first official Preceptor Workshop as one of the Lecturers. I was part of those Preceptor workshops for two years.

I'm grateful to Nate Rosenbaum, our latest Nurse Manager for 4 East, and to my long-time friend and co-worker, Josie, who walked with me through good and hard times.

Finally, I am grateful to all of those people who enriched my life, the ones I precepted from start to finish, the novice RNs, the transitioning RNs, and the nurse educators with special mention to Michelle Goodman and Jane Baltimore, who allowed me to be part of the Preceptor Orientation program at its outset as one of the Lecturers. It was an honor to contribute to that. Thank you to my co-worker RNs, Physical and Occupational Therapists, Hospital Assistants, Social Workers, and Housekeepers. Above all, thank you to all my patients who came and crossed my life, teaching me about life itself and its many paths and challenges. My patients taught me that there is resilience of spirit within each being and that teachers are not necessarily the most educated ones. Our teachers are not necessarily the ones in the white lab coats and scrubs, but the very people who are the recipients of our care—the patients themselves are our "silent teachers" on that side of the bed!

Farewell to 30 years of NURSING My Retirement Letter ~ 2016

My 30 years of employment at Harborview is finally coming to a close as the year 2016 approaches its end. It has been long, compared to the time that most people stay at one place of employment, not to mention the same unit all that time! But it has been such a blessing to me personally and professionally and to my family. It's hard to imagine myself no longer a NURSE, officially. But I think it has been half my life since I turned 62 this year . . . so, it will always be a part of who I am. I have many, many people to thank who I may not be able to see and thank personally. I will thank them in my thoughts and prayers, and I will remember them always through the years. Sandy, my first Nurse

Manager; "Tommie," my mentor and forever professional enthusiast; and Laura Newcomb, my first preceptor, friend, and mentor, who became my Nurse Manager for several years; and you, my last Nurse Manager with whom I close my Nursing career. And, of course, Josie, with whom I worked through the years, my friend forever.

Transitions are always difficult and challenging, but I'm grateful to everyone. Thank you for stepping into this role at a very opportune time when the unit needed someone who could UNIFY the staff. 4 East is an awesome place to be planted, to grow, mature, and then to finally retire from. Harborview, in more ways than one, resembles a mini world full of diverse individuals from healthcare professionals to patients—and I must say, the most colorful sets of patients one could ever imagine! It's been a challenge, a real "life teacher," a REALITY SHOW with real live actors and the staff I have come to know and love . . . It isn't so much the place itself, but the PEOPLE. I will miss it terribly, but not that much!

For now, I plan to do some things in mind. But instead of a TO DO list, I will do a "Maribel list." To walk slowly, not effortlessly, but purposefully . . . to sing and dance with the wind if the WIND is there. To bask in the sun if the SUN is there . . . and if nothing else, to just BE STILL, embrace the moment and let LIFE be . . . and be aware of myself evolving and evolving and evolving . . . Again, thank you for your support in my last years in this place . . . it's been fun, funny, sad, challenging, and always in my heart, it will be a part of me.

Sincerely,

M

Chapter 8

Ecclesiastes

For everything there is a season and a time for every purpose under Heaven.

Ecclesiastes 3:1

 *I*ntroduction

Not everything in life is beautiful. But GOD has an appointed time for every season in our lives.

The varied circumstances that we go through—welcome or not, are part of our own personal journey. The health scares—the life and death situations—are what stand out for me because those were the times that in desperation, I reached out to GOD and went deep into my soul and cried out for help and healing.

Maribel

Part 1

Pain is a great teacher.

For everything there is a season.

Shortly after we moved to our current home in 1997, an unexpected health scare happened to me. The night before going to work, I felt a dull but persistent ache in my abdomen toward the right side of my pelvic region. I took a hot bath with Epsom salts, soaking in it to relax my muscles. Then, I went to sleep. The following morning, I distinctly felt a sharp pain in the same area where I hurt before. I put two fingers to apply pressure on the area to relieve the pain. It helped, so I went to work that way. By afternoon toward the end of my shift, I sat at my computer to chart on my patients. It was then that this incessant pain all of a sudden became immensely unbearable. I was determined to finish my shift, and I planned to go home and rest. Quietly, I worked as tears rolled down my face. My co-worker, who sat beside me noticed and asked, "Are you okay, Maribel?"

I said without turning toward her, "No, Jos, I am in so much pain. I can barely move." With tears continuing to roll down my face, I said, "I have to call my husband to come pick me up. Don't worry, I'll finish and give my report to the next shift." She looked at me with great concern in her eyes.

Just a week prior to this happening, this co-worker of mine told me about her mom who had recently passed away from an undiagnosed cancer, which began with severe abdominal pains, her only symptom. Her mom went to her MD with this complaint. She was assessed completely, and an abdominal ultrasound was done with no conclusive findings. So, of course, she dealt with it by doing nothing. Finally, after several months of feeling this way (with abdominal pain that wouldn't relent), she went back to her MD and told him that something was definitely wrong inside her body. She opted to have an elective surgery called exploratory laparotomy of the abdomen to find out what was really going on inside her body. It wasn't until they opened her up that they found a huge lump hidden behind the organs in her abdomen that couldn't be detected by her abdominal ultrasound. They took several tissue samples for biopsy and found them to indicate stage 4 cancer.

She underwent chemotherapy right away. She took a long leave of absence from work. She never divulged any of this to anyone except close family members. My friend told me about it after her mom passed away.

With this severe adomino-pelvic pain I was experiencing, I couldn't help but think that the worst-case scenario for me would be to have what happened to her mom happen to me.

I finished my shift and called my husband to pick me up from work and take me directly to the Virginia Mason Emergency Room.

I could barely walk for the intense pain that I felt. It was a weekend, and the Emergency Room was quite busy. When I laid flat on the gurney, the pain was still there; however, it abated. They took a special ultrasound. I can't recall what it was called, but they said it was the "state of the art technology in the U.S." It was a CT scan with all the bells and whistles—color-coded to show abnormal cells. They found that I had a huge mass in my right ovary. The obstetrician who examined me said I had to have surgery to remove it, the sooner the better. It was a weekend, so they recommended that I have the surgery first thing on Monday morning. We went home that night somber, uneasy, and uncertain of the future because there was the possibility of this huge mass being cancerous.

All I could think of was my children. What will they do without me? They are still so young! Our youngest was only in the first grade. Three of our six children were still in elementary school, two were in middle school, and our oldest was in high school.

Our family gathered together in the family room in front of the fireplace. "Your Mom is not feeling good. She might have surgery first thing on Monday," Bill told the children. I tried not to alarm them, but I couldn't hide or stop the tears from rolling down my face. We said our Family Prayer. Then our oldest son Billy spoke and said, "Mom, you're going to be okay. You're going to be fine. GOD told me."

In the meantime, my husband spoke with his friend about my urgent condition. This friend informed Bill that his girlfriend (at that time) might be able to help. It wouldn't hurt to listen to a second opinion. This girlfriend of his was very brilliant and knowledgeable about Alternative Medicine. Due to her years of study and personal experience, she consulted Chinese Naturopathic Healing for everything. She did not believe in Allopathic or Western medicine, which focuses on treating symptoms versus treating the root cause. It is important to note that with my background based on Western medicine, I was clearly aware that an urgent condition required urgent attention. Nonetheless, Bill and I both felt it didn't hurt to try her approach especially since if we opted for surgery, it wouldn't happen until after the weekend. We had three days until Monday morning to make up our minds. Patricia (Nick's girlfriend) came to our home the following day. She told Nick to tell us: "Whatever you do, do NOT let them cut you!" meaning NO SURGERY.

I distinctly remembered in one of my basic or fundamental classes on cancer and chemotherapy where the lecturer illustrated on the board a small point of a ballpoint pen and said: "Cancer cells, like all cells, are microscopic; therefore, invisible to the naked eye. This pen point contains numerous cancer cells, which become only visible as they aggressively replicate and form into a mass. Cancer cells are present in the body but do not present a problem until they behave unlike 'normal' cells. They multiply beyond what they are meant to do and start to radically outnumber and overwhelm the normal cells and eventually affect the organ's natural function." Makes sense!

And Patricia's advice made a lot of sense to me: "Whatever you do, do not let them cut you!"

Cutting into the body could potentially release some of these cancerous cells into the bloodstream and I suppose these cells could transfer to other parts of the body through the blood. That's why, I presume, medical doctors strongly recommend chemotherapy after cancer surgeries to ensure that the body is totally free from the cancer. However, in most cases, I have seen as a nurse with 30 years of experience, surgery and chemotherapy really don't annihilate the cancer completely!

Patricia came to our home the following day and set up a treatment plan for me to follow strictly in the next three days. First, we visited the Chinese herbs store in Chinatown and told the Chinese doctor my symptoms. I got the impression that Patricia knew exactly what this doctor was prescribing. Few words and simple and clear instructions were exchanged between the herbalist doctor and Patricia. At home, she immediately went about boiling a pot of water in a small container and put the roots and herbs to boil for a few minutes until the mixture was very dark and concentrated. She made me drink this most bitter concoction I've ever tasted in my life! She said, "Drink until done!"

The Treatment Plan consisted of the following:

1. Avoid solid foods for three days to a week.

2. Drink the bitter tea of medicinal herbs and roots twice a day.

3. Take sips of pure ginseng extract from an ampoule 3 to 6 times a day.

4. Soak in tub of hot water as hot as you can tolerate once a day at night and follow these steps: place 10 drops of hydrogen peroxide in the tub water and stir or mix; with the

entire body in a face-down position and fully submersed except the head, take in deep breaths of air and then slowly exhale under water, allowing bubbles to come up slowly as you exhale; soak and breathe in this way until the water cools down.

5. Apply a poultice to the abdomen wherever it hurts.

The poultice consisted of a mixture of herbs and other ingredients made into a paste and placed directly on the skin over the area of my body that hurt. The poultice was meant both to transfer beneficial ingredients to me and to draw out any toxins through the skin, which happens to be the body's largest organ. In this way, by exerting an osmotic effect, the poultice reduced inflammation, relieved pain, and promoted my healing.

After a few days of this strict dietary regimen, hot water baths with hydrogen peroxide, poultice application, etc., I noticed small bumps blistering out on the surface of my stomach. They were slightly painful pustules from which I could express or squeeze out a little bit of pus and a rice-hard "thing" that came out of the pustules. I would then wipe the area with alcohol briskly to clean and close the teeny tiny-hole from which the solidified "rice-looking thing" came out.

The weekend passed and by the third day, I passed huge clots, followed by a normal-looking menstrual period. I was totally pain-free and healed with Patricia's Alternative Healing method.

Humbled and relieved, I remember crying and thanking GOD for this healing to take place and for being given this wonderful chance to continue to be here to raise my young children.

Patricia also did Past Life Regression Therapy while applying the poultice to my abdomen. She did this for 15 to 30 minutes one-time and the process included guided meditation. I don't know if this did anything for me, but I recall she asked me who I felt closest to and who I looked up to the most in my life.

I told her it was Mama Aning, my maternal grandmother. Interestingly, my physical attachments to not-so-healthy life-styles are closely linked to her habits (see Chapter 3, Retracing My Footsteps).

This event happened in the late 1990s.

GOD plants certain people at different times in our lives to be a guide, a help, and a Blessing to us. Bill's friend, Nick, and his girlfriend, Patricia, certainly were those people.

 *Part 2*

When the student is ready, the Teacher will appear.

Ancient Proverb

*A*bout two years ago, another health scare came to me suddenly—totally unexpected.

In the Book of Ecclesiastes—the Book of Wisdom penned by King Solomon, the son of King David, the cyclic seasons in man's life are described.

After experiencing everything he wished and dreamed of, King Solomon concluded that "everything under the sun is VANITY."

He mentions this word vanity several times throughout this book.

I believe there is a thin line between insecurity and vanity. For a little season two years ago, GOD took away my vanity with ill health. I couldn't wear makeup, paint my nails, wear any jewelry, use perfumes or scented lotions—things I love to do as part of being a girl. I could wear nothing on my skin except special white cotton shirts—everything made me itch. And itches, as is their nature, don't stop at the point of the itch but seem to want to multiply in intensity and spread to other parts of the body.

Here's the run-down of what was happening to me:

My head, face, and hands itched the most and nothing seemed to relieve that. I took oatmeal baths. I even went as far as to put the oats on my scalp and hair, thinking this would keep me from so much discomfort and itchy despair.

I tried all kinds of "all natural" salves and lotions as well as steroid cream (cortisone) and Caladryl, all to no avail. From scratching my scalp so much on the front and temple areas, my skin started oozing clear fluid, and while asleep, the exudate from my scalp seeped down to one side of my face and into my eye area because I was positioned on my side.

When morning came, that side of my face was red, and my eye was nearly swollen shut. When my husband looked at me, he was extremely alarmed. "You've got to stop scratching your face!" "I can't help it," I replied as I tried to hide my face from him. In desperation, I asked my nurse practitioner sister if I should take a small (half-dose) of Benadryl. This helped a lot.

But, as benign as Benadryl is to a lot of people, it caused a series of adverse reactions for me when I got exposed to the sun, which was hard to avoid during the summer when this event happened. Furthermore, I had no clue that the rare side effect of Benadryl was rash due to sun or heat exposure!

Due to taking Benadryl, even a little bit of heat or sun exposure made my face swell up into a moon face. My face was like a bright red balloon—my eyes were so swollen that my eyelids turned upward, and my lips were swollen purple like a dark plum. Basically, my face was totally disfigured, and I didn't look like myself.

My sister, Tess, just happened to call me that particular evening to talk and I told her I wasn't doing well.

She came to our house right away and took my temperature—it was 104! She put ice under my armpits, and she applied several changes of cold washcloths as a compress over my face and changed them frequently. She gave me Tylenol, and when the fever wouldn't come down quickly enough, she worried and asked if I would like to have her take me to the hospital.

I told her, "No. They would finish me up."

So, she kept ministering to me with ice packs and cold washcloths until finally my fever subsided, and I fell asleep.

It was late and dark when she went home with barely any gas in her car! That's what true love does! That's what love looks like!

She then alerted everyone in the family that I was very, very sick.

In the meantime, my husband sent his Naturopathic doctor to see me at our house in person. "Your body is totally inflamed," he told me. "No hot drinks. No hot showers or baths. No sweets. Nothing inflammatory. Throw away all old makeup. Stay hydrated. Cold drinks only. You may need to do a full course of antibiotics to prevent any of the severe rash and infected open skin from going deeper into the next layer of your epidermis. If this happens, you could have erysipelas—an acute bacterial skin infection that affects the dermis layer of skin and can extend to the superficial cutaneous lymphatic system. Such an infection is usually caused by group A Streptococcus bacteria but can also be caused by other bacteria found normally on the skin surface such as Staphylococcus aureus."

And because our hands touch everything and due to the relentless itch, he was worried that I would also spread the bacteria to other parts of my body. Erysipelas is characterized by local inflammation and fever, and I had both of these symptoms.

In my case, I scratched my head, my scalp, my face, my arms, and whatever else I could reach with my ever so busy hands! The wounds on my hands got deep and ugly.

I was miserable to the max! The Lord took away the "crown" on my head slowly but surely and replaced it with a scab. And when I grew impatient with not healing fast enough, GOD put the fear of other possible diagnoses—an autoimmune disorder we desperately did not want to entertain or cross our minds!

I had full blood draws and a special lab test to identify if this unknown illness was some type of autoimmune disease. Because it was ordered "STAT" the results were supposed to come back within 24 hours. When this didn't happen, doubt plagued my mind. I remember thinking, "Oh, my sister and my PCP do not want me to know the results."

♥ It was at this point, from the depths of my soul, I asked GOD to please heal me. I cried and went down on my knees and placed my head and face on the floor in my bathroom sanctuary—my Inner Sanctum.

Three days passed and the lab results came back, and we learned they hadn't labeled the tube "STAT" at all, which was upsetting. But, as GOD would have it, it gave me Time to reflect deeply as my faith got tested and GOD once again listened to my deep prayers of supplication.

The results came back NEGATIVE for an autoimmune disorder, which we had feared initially.

So, I was able to embark on A New Beginning . . .

"Change your DIET, Mom," Moemoe, my youngest daughter said.

"Reset your gut microbiome," a health-nut employee of my husband's said.

"Change your diet, Mom," Charlie said echoing Moemoe.

My daughter, who is also a nurse, drew my blood to test for allergens. Those results came back on point! Everything I over-indulged in I was allergic to: glutens, chicken, salmon, almonds, corn, and egg whites, to name a few!

So, this totally agreed with one of the theories of allergies. That theory is: overexposure to the same substance over a long period of time can cause you to become allergic to it. And, definitely, these foods were what I often overindulged in. I ate almonds daily as a snack, in the raw, roasted, or smoked. I loved crunchy QFC fried chicken—especially the skin. I loved salmon, preferring that to any meat—steak or pork. I hate lamb. I loved eating fried tuna with scrambled eggs mixed in, Filipino-style. I love egg whites versus yolks in hardboiled eggs. I love corn on the cob—I could eat three ears in one sitting all by myself. And, of course, the greatest spoiler of all, gluten-rich breads and pastries! And then there's my daily Starbuck's mocha—which is rich in sugar. This diet finally took its toll and caused my body to become severely inflamed.

I have always prided myself on being a food adventurist. My oldest daughter used to tell me: "Mom, you have the gut of a seagull!" This is because I could eat anything without getting sick, like leftovers, which to us Filipinos (I mean my family, no offense to others!) ate all the time, without any problems.

But this time, at this age, and in this "SEASON" of my life, my body could no longer support such an unhealthy diet!

I was totally miserable, my immune system broke down, my physical appearance totally changed—so something had to CHANGE.

Health is wealth. I had wealth but I couldn't go anywhere to enjoy that wealth. So, it felt like "hell" to be in my condition—like a hungry person staring at an out-of-reach table full of food. I had to change my diet drastically.

No salves or creams could heal me. No medicine. A total change in diet was called for. A GUT reset was the key.

According to current research, roughly 70% to 80% of the immune system is located in the gut. A significant portion of our body's immune cells reside in the gastro-intestinal tract. So, maintaining our gut microbiome with healthy eating is crucial to staying healthy.

OMG! Why didn't I know that? I don't believe it's common knowledge either. Oh, the things we take for granted in life until what's good leaves us and our own bodies betray us and can no longer support us. So, I ordered a special diet called Trifecta prepared from all natural veggies, mostly root vegetables with no seasonings. Eating this food was like eating soft cardboard because it was without the sensational flavors I am used to! I drank only beef broth and alkaline water with micro-electrolytes in it.

I stayed away from the sun or from direct heat from a heater. I did not take hot showers. I felt like I was a prisoner in my own home because I couldn't go out anywhere.

My whole family ministered to me, taking turns, coming to take care of my needs. My husband moved his trumpet lessons to our home so he could be home earlier with me. I could see in his eyes a worried look he couldn't hide despite the fact that I assured him that I was on the mend. He just had to have faith and be patient.

I wore beanie hats for a year to hide my baldness. A few long strands of hair on the back of my head hung more like "nostalgia."

My Mom came to visit me two to three times a week as my sister, Tess, drove her to our house. Mom was pretty frail herself at that age of 92 years. And yes, she was the Best Mother in the World. She was not about to let her own age and frailty keep her away from seeing me.

I remember distinctly my Mom saying, "If Mohammed won't go to the mountain, then the Mountain will go to Mohammed!" as she walked up the front steps to my house supported on each side by Tess and my other sister, Marilyn.

My Dad used to say this when he and Mom would come visit me at our house after not seeing me for a while. Then he would say: "I miss you, Dai." So, I figured Dad was saying this to me through my Mom and was there visiting as well during this time of illness.

My Mom's last visit to me was on a Wednesday—and she died three days later at Evergreen Medical Center shortly after she was ambulanced to the Emergency Room.

Such strength, such resilience, such dignity with which she honored her Motherhood to the very end!

I realized that I could be as strong as her, too. That's who she was and that's who we take after and look up to.

After about a year, my scalp revived and grew wisps of brand new shiny and silvery gray hair. With the Trifecta diet, I lost about 8 to 10 pounds. I consumed no sugar, no sweets, no leftover foods, and no processed foods. Amazing. And on this diet, I lost my craving for "junk foods" and constant oral gratification.

The lessons I gleaned from this experience . . . "to everything there is a season and a special purpose under Heaven":

1. TRUST GOD with every season in your life.

2. Endure to the end. Be patient in the process of healing. We don't know when illness comes to us, or how long it will last. Be <u>patient</u> in the process of <u>waiting</u> for <u>healing</u>.

3. Not everything in life is beautiful externally—but GOD somehow makes and <u>restores everything beautiful in its own Time</u>.

4. There is a thin line between insecurity and VANITY. Be content with how you look. Of course, who doesn't want to look good? It's natural, but do not obsess over external beauty. GOD is more interested in the beauty of your heart and soul.

5. As I know fully well, GOD hears all our prayers in His own Time no matter what season in life we are going through.

GOD blesses us to become a blessing to others who may experience what we've gone through ourselves.

We understand deeply because we know how it feels to walk in their shoes. And, in turn, we extend our help and support to these people. They learn from us as we learned through our own personal experiences. And thus, the cycle of life keeps moving . . .

The cycle of love and compassion is passed on.

♥

I am who I am because GOD is who He is,
and I am made in His image—
"the daughter of a King" who happens to be GOD Himself!

Ecclesiastes 3:1–8, Old Testament

To everything there is a season,

and a time to every purpose under heaven:

A time to be born, and a time to die;

A time to plant, and a time to pluck up, that which is planted;

A time to kill, and a time to heal;

A time to break down and

A time to build up;

A time to weep, and

A time to laugh;

A time to mourn, and

A time to dance;

A time to cast away stones, and

A time to gather stones together;

A time to embrace, and

A time to refrain from embracing;

A time to get, and

A time to lose;

A time to keep, and

A time to cast away;

A time to rend, and

A time to sew;

A time to keep silence, and

A time to speak;

A time to love, and a time to hate;

A time of war, and a time of peace.

For everything there is a season . . .
thus, continue to trust GOD in every season of your life!
♥

Chapter 9

For the Love of Bobby

*F*resh wounds hurt deep, and the pain is so intense that one is unable to see beyond that pain at such a moment.

Fortunately, TIME is a healer. It allows us to sit back, revisit, and reflect on those events when the silt has settled.

It has been three years since our brother, Bobby, passed away in 2021. An untimely death by which everyone in the Family felt so incredibly crushed. This was so totally unexpected, so many regrets to chew upon and recapitulate.

This is Bobby's story . . .

Bobby was a brilliant, young, talented athlete, lawyer, real estate team builder, a counselor, a husband, and a father of three children, whom he loved so much. He was a wonderful human being, the 9th sibling in our family of ten.

Bobby was beloved by many, adored by friends and family. He was a combination of intellect, a tender heart and soul. I remember I could talk to Bobby about spiritual, metaphysical, and scientific things that he understood and was able to relate to. He was open to things—he was analytical but never judgmental. He was really easy to talk to.

In high school, he was quite popular because of his good demeanor and multi-talents (dancing and basketball), which naturally made people gravitate toward him. He was also a hard worker, finding jobs (e.g., college counselor for new students to guide them on their career path) when he was not busy with his own schooling himself.

He had his own law practice at the Pioneer Building in Pioneer Square, downtown Seattle, and later moved to Bellevue to join a well-known law firm.

Bobby's Christian beliefs and conservative values eventually moved him and his family to North Carolina where he sent his kids to a Christian school in an environment where they would find themselves surrounded and immersed in traditional Christian values. Family was very important to him.

Flash forward, which brings me to the reason why I am writing this chapter for my brother. I want to share his story of unfortunate events that lead me to believe he died an untimely death, which could have been averted.

It all began like this . . .

From the story I was told, on August 30th, 2021, Bobby fainted on the floor in his home in North Carolina. His wife called 911 and Bobby was taken to the hospital ER. He was tested for COVID and found to be positive. He was then admitted to the hospital and was informed that he would stay there for at least a couple of weeks.

He called and talked to my sister, Tess, every day. They were close and he made her promise to keep it from the family so people would not unnecessarily worry and stress over him. He said he would fight through this, and he would be fine.

He was immediately placed on continuous oxygen at a setting of 6 liters per nasal canula with the oxygen saturation in the 90s. His other vital signs were stable, but he was short of breath on exertion. He was diagnosed with COVID-pneumonia. The only treatments he was receiving were Dexamethasone, Lovenox (a blood thinner), and oxygen.

Every day, his wife came to the hospital, but she was not allowed to see him in person because of their COVID protocol.

By the end of his first week in the hospital, our whole family was informed that our brother, Bobby, was very sick indeed. Two of my brothers immediately consulted with my husband about what to do.

Bill told them, "Go there to be with Bobby ASAP. It's imperative to be there in person, to make a strong presence of Family, support each other, and provide medical advocacy." At this time, reports of Bobby's progress were uncertain.

To treat his COVID-pneumonia, Bobby received Dexamethasone to decrease inflammation and help with his breathing, continuous oxygen, and Lovenox, which is a standard treatment and medicine for patients who are not so mobile due to illness. As the days passed, Bobby became very uneasy and apprehensive. Bobby verbalized this concern, asking what his patients' rights were by telling us: "I'm getting mixed messages from the doctors and nurses. Which is it?"

He did not feel comfortable being at that hospital because the pneumonia wasn't getting treated. As the days wore on him, his breathing required higher oxygen needs. They gave him morphine IV to ease the labor of breathing. This in turn made him lethargic, weak, and unable to eat or drink much. "Get him out of there!" my husband told my brothers.

I said, "You could leave Against Medical Advice (or AMA)," but his MD said Bobby would not survive the transport. His wife called the closest medical center in the hopes that he would get better care and a better outcome. But she was informed that there were no empty beds. Caught between a rock and a hard place, there was no choice but to have him stay where he was in Wilmington, North Carolina.

My brothers asked Bobby's doctor to start him on intravenous antibiotics to treat the pneumonia and to give him supplemental intravenous fluids with a high dose of vitamin C to keep him hydrated and boost his immune system.

But his doctor said, and this is a direct quote: "No antibiotics. COVID is a virus and will not respond to that. No IV fluids with vitamin C. That is EXPENSIVE urine!" Finally, the doctor refused to give Bobby ivermectin because it had not been approved or proven to work for COVID.

The push from the doctors for Bobby to be moved to the ICU became intense by the second week of his hospital stay despite

Bobby's repeated, vehement refusal to go to the ICU. This annoyed Bobby tremendously. He said, "WHAT DO YOU NOT UNDERSTAND? NO ICU, NO INTUBATION!"

To this day, I am haunted by his reticence or insistence to refuse the ICU and intubation to the very end, as if somehow he knew instinctively he would not make it out of there alive.

The doctor who took over his care after the first team rotation said to my brother, Bong: "I don't blame him for refusing ICU because ICUs these days nationwide have zero success with COVID."

In this case, at least someone listened and was compassionate enough to understand her patient's concern. However, Bobby's oxygen needs increased so that he went from having a nasal canula to a face mask. His condition required more attention than the "regular floor" nurses could provide to meet his needs. The medical staff preached ICU to him, his wife, and family saying that it was his only chance to get better—in the ICU he would have the right equipment to support him and 1:1 nursing care.

Still, at this point, no medical intervention was given to treat the pneumonia, nor was there any practical approach or consideration to boost his immune system and overall health. Clearly, after this long period of time with no nutrition or hydration, he was becoming weaker by the day. In other words, he was left without internal resources to fight this virulent infection.

The unwillingness of doctors to collaborate with the patient and Family's requests to provide intravenous antibiotics to treat his pneumonia and immune-boosting fluids to treat his dehydration, in my opinion, proves a level of negligence and medical arrogance that is contrary to the Hippocratic Oath of "do no harm." Additionally, they failed to do the simple, practical, and common-sense tasks of mobilizing the patient and using frequent incentive spirometry or employing chest physiotherapy by respiratory therapists to help prevent respiratory secretions from settling in his lungs. Not doing these things allowed the pneumonia to proliferate so that his lungs were unable to fully expand and function as they should. In my opinion, all of this "non-patient-centered care" contributed to Bobby's condition getting worse!

We were then told that a critical inflammatory marker (CRP or C-Reactive Protein) was incredibly high, signaling the critical status of the infection in his lungs. The doctors gave him a one-time dose of Sarilumab to attempt to reverse this serious inflammatory process. Sarilumab is very nephrotoxic and using it may result in kidney failure. The following day we were told that Bobby had responded well to the Sarilumab infusion, and his CRP levels had gone down.

My brother said he spoke with Bobby who sounded like he was in high spirits, and Bobby told him he would try to mobilize that day. Pleased with the results, our Family was hopeful that Bobby was on his road to recovery. The following morning, however, Bobby's wife was told he'd had a rough night. He had been dyspneic (short of breath) causing his oxygen levels to drop to extremely low levels. As a result, he was placed on high oxygen via a face mask and given intravenous morphine PRN (or as frequently as needed) to ease his labor of breathing (LOB) through-out the night.

It seemed to me that Bobby's already beleaguered body had been allowed to deteriorate through dehydration and lack of cellular nourishment. Due to pneumonia and COVID, his body became more acidic from lactic acid build up caused by increased tissue breakdown related to infection and his normal bodily functions. Lactic acid build up will cause a critical acid/base imbalance that negatively affects various organs in the body, especially the liver and the kidneys, the body's two filter organs.

In such a condition, initially the body will try to self-correct this acidic condition through the respiratory system by blowing off excess carbon dioxide. To do this, the patient would auto-matically increase his rate of breathing. If that doesn't work, the body attempts to correct the acid/base imbalance through the metabolic system or via the kidneys. However, with excessive tissue breakdown in the absence of hydration and lack of cellular nourishment, the body then goes into crisis mode inundating the two filter organs (the liver and kidneys). Both the liver and the kidneys become unable to detoxify the blood in the midst of an already critical illness. Without preventive and prompt corrective measures (e.g., continuous IV hydration and treatment of infec-tion), septicemia (a bacterial blood infection) will ensue.

If still allowed to continue, the body becomes further compromised and the inflammatory process goes on overdrive leading to generalized sepsis (blood poisoning due to an infection).

By Friday of his second week of hospitalization, through much coercion from medical staff and family, Bobby, who was still able to think and speak for himself, finally, conceded against his own initial inner instinct. He was transferred to ICU by Saturday afternoon. Within 24 hours, he was intubated. This meant that he could no longer speak for obvious reasons, and he was no longer able to move because of chemical restraint. But immediately, prior to the procedure, he asked: "Intubate? Intubate?" asking the family for confirmation.

Then he spoke his last mortal words to his loved ones: "Okay. I'm going under. I love you guys."

The following Sunday morning, our family received a critical call from our brothers who were at the hospital with Bobby.

The doctors said: "He can go anytime."

Bobby's wife and kids were allowed to go into the ICU and be with our brother as he was dying. They watched all his vital signs displayed on the monitor. His body was racked with extreme fever (over 40°C/104°F). He was breathing hard with his oxygen saturation and level of blood oxygen plummeting.

Countless prayers of faith and desperation were offered. We all supplicated for the GOD of Mercy to give us a miracle of healing. By the end of Sunday, Bobby had recovered miraculously. His vital signs were better, and his blood oxygen was in the high 90s. His fever had come down.

Finally, a bag of continuous intravenous fluids and antibiotics was started!

That Sunday evening, his ICU doctor informed his wife and family that they needed to put Bobby on dialysis. And so, a hemodialysis catheter was inserted via the femoral artery to obtain vascular access. However, dialysis did not start until very early Tuesday morning. Later, we were informed that Bobby's dialysis catheter became occluded and attempts to dissolve the clot were unsuccessful. The staff gave up and did not pursue solving the problem.

On Tuesday, approximately 4 am Seattle time, we received an emergency call from Bobby's wife, who asked us to say something to our brother, Bobby, on the phone. We were being asked to say our goodbyes.

We took turns as she put her cellphone next to his ear. Again, we heard the doctor say: "He can go anytime now."

Bill exclaimed with expletives: "Don't let him go! Do everything you can do to keep him from dying!"

Then, our family in Washington immediately set up a Zoom call so we could view our brother Bobby live. On Zoom, we watched our brother's condition decline rapidly. I noticed his face turning somewhat dusky. The monitors were displaying unfavorable vital signs and hypoperfusion (decreased blood flow in the organs).

The nurse explained that they had a problem with the dialysis catheter clotting and getting occluded and were therefore unable to dialyze him. Our family saw on Zoom that Bobby was no longer getting intravenous fluids to support his declining system. When we asked why there was no IV, the nurse confirmed, "No. There's no IVF." When we asked, "Why not?" She replied, "The doctor did not order it."

Bobby's immediate family were surrounding him in his ICU bed. Then, his daughter, who was near the foot of his bed touched his feet and said, "He's cold." She knew, and she excused herself from being in her Dad's room. Bebot came in to replace her (only a limited number of people was allowed in a patient's room) and immediately he asked the nurse to bring warm blankets to warm our brother's body. At this point, as I watched, this dreadful thought came to my mind: "he is shunting." This happens when blood flow gets redirected away from the extremities to vital organs during shock. Bebot then asked the nurse to call Bobby's ICU doctor as soon as possible. Mind you, Bobby was still a full code (meaning all life-saving measures should be taken), but the medical staff did not respond immediately.

When the doctor answered the call, Bebot asked, "Please, please, sir, can you give Bobby a bolus of IV fluid with high dose vitamin C?" The doctor calmly informed him that the hospital does not carry that in their formulary. Then, Bebot got our other doctor on the phone and asked what dosage to give Bobby. Finally, after much pleading, the ICU doctor conceded and said, "I'll order it, but it takes time for our pharmacy to fill this request."

"Please, sir," Bebot said. "Time is of the essence. We do not have time to wait. Time is not on our side."

Meanwhile, Bobby's vital signs and blood oxygen levels were continuing to decline. The family assisted the ICU nurse in putting warm blankets on Bobby's core and feet to keep him warm and comfortable.

We, our Family, were keenly aware that the time of no turning back was clearly evident.

Bobby's blood pressure was 37/27, his heartrate was very slow, his blood oxygen was very low, and he still had extreme hypoperfusion. His body was shutting down and near death. He was at this point very septic, a point of no return—Bobby died after being "coded" one more time with the paddles, etc.

In my opinion, this did not have to end this way! Bobby could have been saved from the vile consequences of infection had the doctors moved early on during his hospitalization to treat the pneumonia. Prophylactic intravenous antibiotics for a presumptive bacterial infection and intravenous hydration to maintain cellular maintenance and organ integrity especially for the kidneys, I feel, would have positively curved the course of Bobby's illness.

We know someone personally here in Washington who was admitted for COVID-pneumonia. She was given IV fluids and IV antibiotics while in the Emergency Department right away. She recovered after a few days and went home alive!

To put it simply & boldly, Bobby died from COVID-pneumonia because of:

1. No treatment initiated or sustained presumptively or not,

2. No continuous supportive or supplemental hydration,

3. No cellular nourishment for a prolonged period of time of about two weeks, and

4. Ensuing sepsis without corrective measures and this condition eventually killed him.

I believe Bobby died an untimely death. What could have been a preventable outcome became an inevitable pathway to decline. By reading Bobby's story, anyone can surmise where the "gap" happened.

I've shared Bobby's story with a few of my friends and Family members. I find that indeed his story is relevant and echoes the experience of others. Bobby's story is not an isolated incident but is commonplace across the country.

We will not be silent nor be silenced. The country needs to look into this, and hospitals badly need an institutional ENEMA if we are to solve this and other devastating illnesses. A country without its people, due to them dying unnecessarily, is not a nation but a desperate land that will soon become desolate if allowed to continue unchecked.

For the LOVE of Bobby, share your loved ones' experiences in relation to this pandemic. Ignite the flame of AWARENESS so healing will take place.

Love U Bobby,

Sis Maribel

10/22/21

My Mom on Mother's Day

Chapter 10

All About My Mom

~ A Godly woman according to the Bible ~

She is clothed with strength and dignity; she can laugh at the days to come. She speaks with WISDOM, and on her tongue is the law of kindness. She watches over the affairs of her household and does not eat the bread of idleness.

Many women do noble things, but you surpass them all.

Proverbs 31:25–27 & 29

Charm is deceitful, and beauty vain, but a woman who fears the LORD, she shall be praised.

Proverbs 31:30

*W*hat comes to mind when I think about my Mom?

When I think about her, I see her beautiful face, her strength, her resilience, her energy, her determination, her deep faith in GOD, her dedication to family, her love of throwing big parties and decorating, her love of redecorating her home according to the seasons. She never got tired. Even in bed, her mind was always busy; looking around at the ceiling and the walls, she would see even the littlest cobwebs, or dust, and she would point that out. Everything had to be clean and in order. She was a meticulous woman in everything she did. Her presence was so distinct that you would know when she left the room that she had been there!

She was not the kind of woman who would lay around in sweats or pajamas all day, drink coffee or tea, and watch TV.

She did all that at the end of her day. Then, she never failed in her nightly routine of cleaning her face and moisturizing—maybe this is why she kept her youthful look even to the very end—of her mortal life—in her 90s.

Mom was always on-the-go. She loved going out to eat, shopping, traveling, or just tagging along with my sister, Tess, wherever she went. She loved brand name clothing, bags, shoes, and even brand name foods! Unlike me who enjoys "junking" or going to thrift stores and Dollar Tree, she enjoyed the finest things in life.

She loved eating out and one of her favorites was the hot crab sandwich at Burgermaster by Children's Hospital on Sandpoint Way. We used to stop by there on our way home from her job at University Hospital Medical Center before she retired as an anesthesia tech and while I was going to college at the University of Washington.

She traded this treat for Doritos and Coke later in her life when she was homebound.

In the 1980s, I remember after having dinner and cleaning up, all of us girls would go to our parents' bedroom and watch our favorite show, *Dallas*. She would have a cup of one of her favorite General Foods International Coffee flavors—"Café Vienna" or "Café Français"—with orange-chocolate-flavored Pepperidge Farm Milano cookies. She enjoyed this special time with only us girls.

She had a total of 10 children, six boys and four girls, and she was very proud of that. Her greatest life mission and accomplishment was as a wife and mother of ten. Being a mother was her greatest joy and pride, and she kept us all together through thick and thin.

Her other favorite thing in life was getting nightly massages from us, her children. Vicks and Bengay were always on her nightstand beside her bed.

"Mommy-La"
My Mom celebrating her and my Dad's 50th Wedding Anniversary

When she was younger or in her younger years, I remember that she would send for her masseuse, Manding Victoria, an elderly lady with a slightly bent back. This little lady had strong brown hands. She would come to our house with her self-concocted potion of some type of oil and crushed ginger, which she put in a little sack the size of her palm. The sack material looked like it was made from cheesecloth, which she warmed up, so when she massaged, only the hot oil would go on my Mom's skin and not the ginger.

Mom loved it, and it seemed as if Manding Victoria did this for hours until my Mom fell asleep. Her fees were placed at the nightstand, ready for her to collect, so she wouldn't have to wake my Mom up. And, before leaving, she would help herself to a hot cup of cocoa and a roll. Then, the little, old masseuse lady would be walked back to her home by one of our maids.

Mom was a natural born leader, much like my Dad. Although she was quiet and shy as a young girl, she took on my Dad's qualities as a public figure over their years together. She was the "Queen Bee" of all the Bees my Dad used to say.

And she fulfilled that role very well with class and dignity. She was not always patient with us children. She had to crack her whip a few times as one would have to do, I suppose, with such a big pack of 10. We all respected her authority and loved her to the very end.

One of my most treasured memories of her was when I got so ill in 2022. I couldn't leave the house, so she made sure she came to visit me and said, "If Muhammed won't go to the mountain, the mountain will go to Muhammed!" My Dad used to say this. The last time she came to visit me was on a Wednesday, three days before she passed away. She was the greatest mom to the very end.

I mourned when she passed away, of course, but there was something so different and special with her passing. It was as if she just "stepped into the next room"! It was as if it was just her natural time to go. Her passing made it easy for me to mourn and not grieve indefinitely because she truly did live to the fullest and did her very, very best. She had no regrets and enjoyed a life lived very well. In the end, she had a total of over thirty grandchildren! It's amazing what a world of people, what a community, can come from one individual, tiny woman!

Love you, Mom, forever!

Chapter 11

Inner Sanctum

Let the imaginations
of your heart flow freely
through your fingertips,
& let your pen walk
a thousand miles
with you sitting down in one place.

By MB Cahill

*O*ver the years journaling has been a favorite pastime of mine. I find comfort in the QUIET inspiration that comes when no one is around to interrupt my thoughts.

While others may seek counseling to sort out their thoughts and right their busy anxious-laden lives, I prefer the company of no one & delve deep into my very own soul.

In the presence of much company, my easily distracted self gets wound up & unable to focus. This practice of journaling really helps me unload any kind of negative baggage I may have picked up during the day.

As a result, although I never worked the night shift, I have become a true night owl for nighttime is <u>a time of silence</u> & <u>my sweet INNER SANCTUM</u>. ♥

My definition:

Inner sanctum means a quiet place, a sanctuary, a sacred place, a refuge, a retreat, a hide away in which no one is allowed to enter.

Google's definition:

Inner Sanctum

- the most sacred place in a temple or a church
- a private or secret place to which few other people are admitted

- a room which is private and sometimes secret, where one can be QUIET & ALONE
- a refuge, retreat, den, hideaway
- synonyms: sanctuary or shrine

Part 1
Reflections Through
Journal Writing

My Inner Sanctum
When the ways of the world crowd me
When the demands of those around me
and my immediate surroundings of clutter and accumulations
threaten to overwhelm me,
I run to GOD's Word (the Scriptures), journal my thoughts down,
and here He straightens me up and strengthens me.

MBCahill

*L*ong before journal writing was fashionably advocated by many professional counselors or church leaders, I embraced it as part of my daily routine. I have done so ever since my kids were young. My days were long and exhausting, and I took to journal writing as a "fish longs for water to swim in in order to survive." It provided an outlet for me to download my hectic busy life as a wife, mother, and a full-time nurse at a busy hospital.

Don't get me wrong—life was full and fulfilling, but also physically and emotionally challenging. It is only in looking back at those earlier years by revisiting my old journals that I recognize the precious experiences I had and the lessons I received became a big part of who I am today. This reminds me of what Ralph Waldo Emerson penned: "The years teach us much which the days never knew." How true this is. As there is no time to reflect on the simple things we did each day, which were the things that mattered most at the time. It is a wonder how we survived those busy years.

To this day, I write in my journals. Perhaps there are at least 50 or more I have gathered through the years. The most profound entries are those written with a broken heart and tears—all revolving around my immediate family. I often address the Lord GOD in those entries, making them more like prayers or conversations with GOD Himself. He (GOD) answers me back through my thoughts and I write down His messages to me personally as if He were right there but, of course, I cannot see Him!

GOD has been good to me. I always say to my children, "GOD is the one who knows us best and loves us most." I believe this truly with all my heart, and my belief has given me confidence that everything, no matter what, will work out for the best because I am in GOD's hands, and He is in control.

I am now in a different phase in my life. The "gathering phase" I call it. All the events and experiences along the way are scattered pearls throughout our lifetime. It is time to gather them and string them together to make an offering to the One who gave me life and gave me my life's companion and blessed us both with our six beautiful children.

Psalm 127:3 Children are a heritage of the Lord,
the fruit of the womb is His reward.

Heritage refers to an inheritance or blessing. Children are gifts from GOD; they are a blessing to the family and are a unique blend of their parents.

As such, we love them all and each individually. They truly are unique in their own individual personalities and struggles in life. As parents, we did the best we could and knew how to do to provide for their basic needs. We may not always have been there for them all the time. But in the end, I hope they know that we tried to do the best we could and knew how. I love you and will Forever. ♥ Mom

Part 2
A Collection of My
Inspired Prose and Poetry

Sunday Afternoon

A song of glory
A song of Love,
    I sing voiceless—nonetheless,
    I feel it in my heart.
I connect with . . .
    the ONE who made me,
    carved out from His very own Heart.
My thoughts rise out & above toward Heaven.
He is there.
Yet, He is also here inside my head and heart.
Is that what it means to be connected
    to this SOURCE of LIFE where I came from?
The very SOURCE of LIFE from whom
    everyone & EVERYTHING come from.
When I am connected to this SOURCE of LIFE,
    I am at PEACE.
    I am calm.
    I am comforted &
    I float in the ether that envelopes
        ALL the good feelings in LIFE.
    I am grateful & my soul is FULL! ☺ ❤

3/12/23
MBCahill❤

The Vivacious Tongue
(a word of advice)

When one sinks deep into one's soul,
the heart opens up like a flower
& begins to sing . . .
a sweet lament of years' muted sounds,
stolen, off-staged by a
vivacious tongue . . .
like noisy cymbals & drums
in a practicing band—
a racket of notes bouncing
off the walls, ceilings, & floors
There is no harmony in tunes
played on their own or wagging tongues
like rivaling instruments seeking
self-recognition in a music
racket-filled room.
Such is the world we live in—
too noisy . . . & afraid of the SILENCE within!
For we might by chance
hear the "STILL small voice"
from whence we came.

3/9/06
MBCahill♥

The Song of the Wind

There is a nostalgic lament
    in this relentless song of the WIND.
"I cannot be seen," It says,
"But I can be heard & felt.
You may ignore me,
But you cannot escape me . . .
For I am HERE & I am the same
    as in the ancient days.
I've seen people in past ages.
I've traveled the desert lands &
crossed the oceans all over.
I've ravaged through rain forests
    & big cities alike.
I AM WIND & though no one sees me,
    nor feels my feelings, I AM real.
I am here as I was & have been.
Though you cannot see me,
You see my effect on everything I touch.
Here I AM & there I AM.
I am here. Hear Me, touch me, &
acknowledge my presence,
my loneliness, my pain.
Hear me, I just want you to acknowledge me.

I am the WIND, which you cannot see,

BUT I AM HERE. HERE I AM." ☹

Hear me.

Note: The wind howls outside my bathroom window, trees swishing to & fro. It doesn't stop.

2/10/06
MBCahill❤

Winter's Last Kiss

March is a gloomy time for many—I know it is for me. The weather's ambivalence plays havoc on my tired old body.

Winter lingers like an unwanted ghost, reluctant to let go.

Winter clings like a worn-out hide.

Spring is hiding & cannot yet make up its mind—

"Is it my Time?" "Is it my turn?"

The rains come & the sun stretches forth its hibernating rays.

"So early," Spring says sleepily.

"I have yet a season to hide—"

So, the poor little lilies, tulips, & crocuses crawl back into their warm little blanket of earth.

Winter's breath too chilly to endure, like unwelcome frost on naked limbs—it bites & then it kills.

Spring WAKE UP!

Yes, it is YOUR Time!

It is your turn! ☺

3/9/06

MBCahill ♥

The Birth of Winter

Like browning leaves in the Fall
ripped apart in the tumultuous rain
& wretched winds—

leaving bare sullen branches,
blackened stiff in the wake of a
coming chill, —that's how I feel.

Old Man Winter comes first with a chill
in his Breath that blows deep into
my bones.

A day begins without permission from the night before,
garbed in its black shroud as if to hide its cold
& unfeeling face—

Ah yes, Old Man Winter, I know you're
here & so am I.

No shroud nor blackened veil can hide
your face; for I feel YOU (!)
even before I see your presence
in this Time & Space.

10/22/02
MBCahill♥

Autumn 2002

A poem I wrote inspired by the beauty of GOD'S Creation
(on my drives to & from work on the SE May Valley Hywy & beautiful Coal
Creek Pkwy)

Life's passing . . .
season's cycle ending.

Farewell to those above the Earth
Vibrant hues of a Golden Time
slowly fading in the rain.

Bared branches like fingers, arms, & Hands
outstretched—
shredded garments of orange & gold
now, lay adorn the ground.

A beauty lives on for just a little while
Now present only in the memory
of the mind.

11/02
MBCahill♥

An inspiration on picking the rune of "The Divine"

I am empty,
yet I am full

I am nothing,
yet I am All

I am space,
with no boundaries
Yes, I am space & limitless

I am space within Time,
yet, I am timeless,
for Time is mine
(last verse added later on 1/19/03)

10/5/02
MBCahill❤

What Was All That About?

A sudden gust of angry wind came in a hurry, loud & fast. I felt it beat against the window—it was really weird. Then, it was gone just like that!

Got up & looked out my bathroom window. There was nothing but hail, wind, & rain—a very visible dusting of hail left in its wake & a few broken off branches lay scattered on my driveway & street. Yes. That was real & not imagined!

2024
MBCahill♥

Chapter 12

Kintsugi:
The Art of Transformation

A pain-free life is great.
But one needs to experience pain
in order to appreciate the
sweetness of a pain-free life.
It is human to complain.
It is human to become complacent
when things are good.
But it is dull & senseless to merely
"slob along" through life without
intention & real consciousness—
a purpose-driven life is best.
So, complain if you must,
but don't stay there! Catch yourself
when complacency creeps in your life
like an insidious smoke seeping
through the little cracks underneath
the unsealed doors of your soul.

By MBCahill

Kintsugi is more than just an art of repairing old broken pottery. In life it has come to symbolize the act of repairing broken relationships, of binding together the past with the present, or healing old wounds, which should not be left to fester, but to REFRESH, RENEW, and REVIVE a beautiful thing that otherwise would have been lost or discarded.

From a Google search for The Origins of Kintsugi:

"Kintsugi is a 15th century practice of repairing pottery, which means, 'To join with gold.' This originated during the Muromachi period in Japan under the Shogunai military regime."

Whether it's a legend or not, no one really knows—the story goes like this: A 15th century military ruler of Japan named Ashikaga Yoshimasa sent one of his tea bowls back to China to be repaired. When it was returned, he was disappointed with the finished product and asked a local craftsman to find a more aesthetic way of repairing his tea bowl. This craftsman found a better solution by combining local tree sap and shimmering gold dust as a binding agent to fix the breakage beautifully.

Another name for Kintsugi is kintsukuroi. It is a laborious process of sanding, smoothing, and mending the areas of breakage in the pottery with urushi lacquer. It is derived from the sap of the urushi tree (*Rhus verniciflua*) mostly found in East Asia. Urushi lacquer is durable enough to last several thousands of years because it is resistant to both acid and alkali environments.

Over time, this traditional method of repairing broken ceramics has evolved to mean something deeper and more powerful—a symbol for HEALING & EMBRACING the beauty of our human imperfections. It is therefore a true art of TRANSFORMATION.

Quotation from The Philosophy of Kintsugi in Mental Health, copied from "Kintsugi in the ART of Transformation":

"Our character is built through the struggles and obstacles we go through in life and our past does not define who we are."

The philosophy of Kintsugi teaches us to reconnect to the lost parts of ourselves that were fragmented and broken during traumatic experiences and emerge fully transformed.

From 2 Corinthians 12:9 (KJV):

His strength is "made perfect in weakness."

From the article in Class Bento (www.classbento.com.au) titled "What Kintsugi Taught Me About Life, Love, and Healing" by Laine Fullerton:

"Share your healing journey: Society has conditioned us to cover our scars and conceal our struggles. Kintsugi, however, goes against the grain and brings these flaws into focus."

Our lives are constantly changing and since no matter how similar in likes or dislikes we may be, somehow we find cracks in each other's character, giving room to either flourish in our relationships or die in drought for lack of care and deeper understanding of each other. Like tending a garden, it takes effort to build a relationship. We can wish and pray in idealistic thinking or live with doom and die in forever daily complaining. Finding faults is never the answer because what we seek, we will find! That's all there is to it. Always, always, it is an active choice.

Everyone experiences hardships and breaks along life's journey. KINTSUGI teaches us to embrace what comes our way—the good as well as the bad because it's what makes us who we are today.

With WISDOM, we learn to discern what is "fluff" and what is real. Separate the kernel from the chaff. See with the eyes of your soul what is here to abide and what is here just passing by.

A Kintsugi master says:

> *"Not all things in life can be mended with bright gold seams, but Kintsugi reminds us that <u>no matter how broken you may feel</u>, with PATIENCE, hard work, long suffering, and ACCEPTANCE, you will somehow soon become WHOLE again."*

So, try to stay optimistic when things seem to dull or fall apart— remember to embrace the flaws and mistakes in life. Forgive yourself, love yourself. <u>Forgive others, love others through the Divine Maker's Eyes</u> (not your own limited self!).

ENDURE * GROW * TRANSFORM and try your best to be the "best you can be"!

What Kintsugi teaches us is to be strong and resilient. We can turn adversity into triumph. Find joy in what we do—even the simple and mundane can become points of greatness. <u>As Mother Theresa says: "We cannot all do great things, but we can do small things with great love</u>."

Like a lot of people, I've taken to social media and have found some gold nuggets I love and like to pass on. Here is one of them I find quite true and relevant—and may benefit some of the readers.

"If you see a married couple still in love through the years, you may think how lucky they are. But in marital relationships, there is no such thing as luck. They've made many compromises; they've overlooked each other's faults. They forgave many mistakes and endured many problems along the way. They spent years learning to understand each other. Love has never been a matter of luck. It's mutual giving, compromise, shared dreams, care, respect, mercy, and patience." [posted by Laura Phelps Sundrla, administrator for INSPIRED, a public Facebook group]

I suppose these are the ingredients of True Love—the only FORCE in the universe that transcends TIME and SPACE and endures Forever . . .

It has been said and written in the Bible that our life is recorded in Heaven in GOD's Book of Life (see Revelation 20:12).

I believe that. All the good, the bad, the right steps, and the missed steps (i.e., mistakes) we took were and are all part of our journey in this mortal life. And I accept that. That is what makes us who we are today. Lessons taught and learned were meant to be there. It is what makes this life so precious and individually, uniquely, our own—a continuing process of evolution of character, which ascends us to our higher selves. These lessons teach us to be humble, to be compassionate, to be grateful, to be empathetic toward others. We are special, and peculiar, yet not exclusive, meaning we are no better or higher than others.

In the Eyes of the ONE Higher than ourselves, from whom we came, we are all the same—made in His image—seeking joy and fulfillment.

As in the ART of KINTSUGI, broken vessels are not discarded, cracks and imperfections are no longer hidden but accepted and made new with the binding lacquer of LOVE, FORGIVENESS, and COMPASSION. It is a new life we embrace and out of it comes PEACE, LOVE, and a deeper UNDERSTANDING of who we are, who others are, what life is about, and what truly matters.

In this world, there is no perfection—only TRANSFORMATION —a process of nature, <u>evolving like a butterfly's humble beginnings</u>. From a mere caterpillar, then wrapped in a plain-looking cocoon, and later to become a butterfly in its resplendent beauty—Free to be who it was ALWAYS meant to Be!

So, like KINTSUGI honors the history of a broken piece of pottery, <u>WE too can honor our own personal struggles and history</u>. We discover ourselves as unique individuals, beautiful in our own way, born to live here TODAY till Forever!

To those of us who have fallen short of our own "perfection"— those who have been through the ringer or rigors of life, as long as we realize we are still beautiful and special in spite of everything, let's give honor to the ONE who truly understands what we've been through and recognize that <u>we are still in the process</u>

of GROWING and BECOMING, who sees beyond the external and sees the BEAUTY of the light that shines within each one of us . . . This is WHO we are—there is a "Velveteen Rabbit" inside each of us. Never mind those who don't understand because truly Beauty lies in the EYES of the BEHOLDER!

From *The Velveteen Rabbit* by Margery Williams Bianco:

"'It doesn't happen all at once,' said the Skin Horse. 'You become. It takes a long time. That's why it doesn't happen often to people who break easily, or have sharp edges, or who have to be carefully kept. Generally, by the time you are REAL, most of your hair has been loved off, and your eyes drop out and you get loose in the joints and very shabby. But these things don't matter at all, because once you are REAL you can't be ugly, except to people who don't understand."

From *The Fourth Instinct: The Call of the Soul* by Arianna Huffington:

"So, if we can be COURAGEOUS one more time than we are fearful, TRUSTING one more time than we are anxious, COOPERATIVE one more time than we are competitive, FORGIVING one more time than we are vindictive, LOVING one more time than hateful, we will have taken the next step in the evolution of our species—and we will have found a new PEACE and MEANING to our lives."

~*The End*~

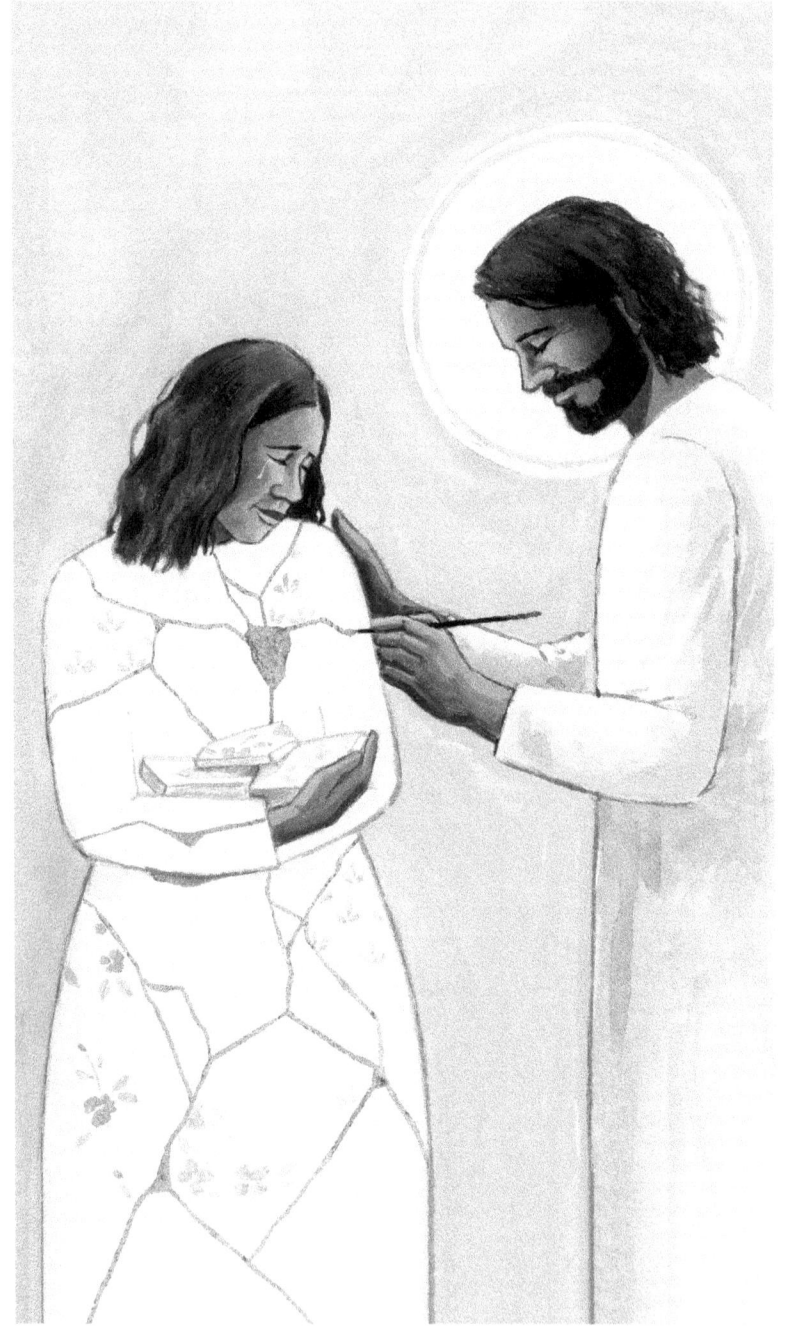

Acknowledgments

Thank you, Heavenly Father,
Lord Jesus Christ, the
author & finisher of my faith.
To my Dad, my Mom, my Honey Bill,
& all of our six children —
you are who made me who
I am today ♥
Thank You all so much!

Maribel

www.ingramcontent.com/pod-product-compliance
Lightning Source LLC
Chambersburg PA
CBHW051510120626
46551CB00012B/852